Young Kate

YOUNG KATE

Christopher Andersen

**MACMILLAN
LONDON**

First published in the United States of America, 1988, by
Henry Holt and Company, Inc., New York

First published in the UK 1988 by
MACMILLAN LONDON LIMITED
4 Little Essex Street London WC2R 3LF
and Basingstoke

Associated companies in Auckland, Delhi, Dublin, Gaborone, Hamburg, Harare, Hong Kong, Johannesburg, Kuala Lumpur, Lagos, Manzini, Melbourne, Mexico City, Nairobi, New York, Singapore and Tokyo

British Library Cataloguing in Publication Data

Andersen, Christopher
    Young Kate.
    1. Cinema films. Acting. Hepburn, Katharine
    I. Title
    791.43'028'0924

    ISBN 0-333-48606-4

Printed by Richard Clay Ltd, Bungay, Suffolk

FOR KIT

Contents

Foreword

It has been my privilege to have known Katharine Hepburn for twelve years, and to have become her friend. That is why it struck me as odd that so many books have been written about her by people whom she insists she has never even met, much less spoken with. (The well-known exception is Garson Kanin, her longtime friend, neighbor, and co-worker on such film classics as *Adam's Rib* and *Pat and Mike* whose bestselling 1971 memoir *Tracy and Hepburn* caused a temporary if painful rift in their relationship.)

Kate, the only name her friends call her, insists that she never reads these books. As she once told me, "I don't read any of the stuff because it would make me very mad, and I don't like to get very mad. Phyllis [her longtime secretary Phyllis Wilbourn] reads them. She's much more tolerant than I am." When one of these biographies came out in the mid-eighties and instantly rocketed up the bestseller lists, Hepburn was nonplussed. "She didn't know me at all," Kate said of the author. "NOT AT ALL. It's ALL newspaper clippings and it's all cockeyed."

"She never talked to you?"

"Wanted to. Said she was going to write a book about me, and I said I don't want to have one written."

"I'm just curious—why?"

"Because they screw it up. They don't tell it the way it happened . . ."

The four-story Manhattan brownstone behind the wrought-iron fence is virtually indistinguishable from its neighbors in the elite East Side enclave of Turtle Bay. But once inside, there is no doubt who lives here. On the wall to the immediate right of the door hang two framed *New Yorker* cartoons. One, a George Price drawing, circa 1935, depicts a filly haughtily tossing her mane while two mares look on enviously. "Oh, she's been acting that way all day," says one mare to the other. "Someone told her she looks like Katharine Hepburn." The other drawing, of post-*On Golden Pond* vintage, depicts a sour-faced elderly couple rocking on the front porch. "You're right," smirks the woman. "I'm *not* Katharine Hepburn—and you're no Hank Fonda, either." No one is more amused by these cartoons than the lady of the house. After a bravura reading of both captions, she renders her verdict. "A real hoot, don't you think?" Kate laughs. "I love them!"

In the downstairs kitchen, Hepburn's longtime housekeeper Norah Moore (hired in part because she was the only job applicant polite enough to stand up when Kate entered the room) is probably cooking up something to satisfy her employer's hearty appetite. Kate is partial to breakfasts in bed (at 6 A.M. she goes downstairs to the kitchen and returns to her bedroom carrying a tray heaped with food), light lunches (Jerusalem artichoke soup served with chipped beef on toast, perhaps, or watercress sandwiches), afternoon tea with biscuits, and early suppers. Forget restaurants. "The food is lousy, and the prices! You pay me sixty dollars," she tells me, "and I'll be happy to fix dinner for you right here."

Kate seems to be in constant motion, forever straightening out pictures on the wall, opening and closing shutters, bending over to realign yet another Persian rug that has gone astray. Kate answers the phone after a single ring. "Miss Hepburn's not here right now," Kate

---

says in that unmistakable voice. "This is the maid. May I take a message?" She then climbs briskly up the steep stairway to the sunlit second-floor living room, where high windows face a shaded rear courtyard she shares with Broadway composer Stephen Sondheim, Garson Kanin (though he sublet his townhouse to a United Nations diplomat following the death of his wife, actress Ruth Gordon), and a few less-famous neighbors. A flaming fragment of log suddenly tumbles from the fireplace out into the room, and without hesitation she gets up and kicks it back in. "I lead," she sighs, "*such* a glamorous life."

The house where Hepburn has lived for nearly sixty years is all comfortable, overstuffed sofas, spindle-legged antiques and ladderback chairs. Each room overflows with bric-a-brac: a gilt-framed mirror over the fireplace, a needlepoint unicorn, a ceramic Buddha headrest, a Victorian birdcage brimming with dried blossoms, two small lacquer boxes depicting snowy scenes from Imperial Russia, a massive chunk of quartz, a game of Chinese checkers, a slab of petrified wood, a Steuben pelican, a pitted cannonball. On a side table there is a striking early portrait by John Singer Sargent of Kate's friend Ethel Barrymore, on another a silver-framed photograph of Kate and Laurence Olivier in a scene from their Emmy-winning television movie *Love Among the Ruins* (when I told Olivier over lunch at London's Savoy Hotel that this photo occupied a place of honor in Kate's living room, his face lit up). In 1987 she sold her most valuable painting, a splashy Vlaminck seascape, and in its place now hangs a moody canvas depicting fishermen on a stormy beach. Atop the mantel is a chimerical creation of Hepburn's own: a thumb-sized bronze cherub lounging on a jagged shard of emerald-green glass. A recent favorite is a bizarre, larger-than-life-sized cast-iron head that, Kate delightedly insists, "looks just like me."

Amidst all this, Hepburn's record four Academy Awards (for *Morning Glory, Guess Who's Coming to Dinner, The Lion in Winter,* and *On Golden Pond*) are nowhere to be seen; they are on exhibit at the Empire State Building in New York. Nor are any of her Emmys displayed. However, it is hard to miss the rather weird-looking, Oscar-sized chrome figure of a woman standing next to the drawing of Ethel Barrymore. This surreal sculpture is her "Lifetime Achievement Award" from the Council of Fashion Designers of America. Kate holds the statuette up and examines it. "Can you imagine?" says Kate, who seldom deviates from her wardrobe of slacks, clogs, turtlenecks and the occasional slouchy hat. "Winning a fashion award for not giving a damn about clothes? Absolutely hilarious."

She may call herself a "rank amateur," but Hepburn is in fact an accomplished artist, both painter and sculptor. Her best paintings are of the lighthouses and marshes at Fenwick, the tiny coastal community in Connecticut where she has summered since the age of five. Yet her most difficult subject, she admits, was not a landscape, but a person. "He had the most magnificent lion's head," says Kate, gazing at the two-inch-high bronze bust she sculpted of Spencer Tracy. "God knows I am no professional, but I think I managed to capture the shape." Painting Tracy was another matter. Although she has painted "dozens of portraits of the people in my life—friends and family, mostly," Kate concedes that "for some mysterious reason I could never quite paint Spencer's face. Oh, I could paint his form, the way he sat, the way he held himself. But that face— there's something about it. So when I painted him reading, I hid his face behind a newspaper."

As Tracy knew all too well, Kate is not reluctant to express her opinions on every conceivable topic from marriage ("I don't give a damn about marriage, but I do care about honor") and children ("I would have made a terrible parent. The first time my child didn't do what I wanted, I'd kill him") to change ("The pendulum may swing back, but first somebody has to push it") to sex in the movies ("If they'd asked me to do a sex scene when I was young, I'd have spit in their eye") to the best way to take a shower (see page 130).

No matter what the subject, she always comes back to her family and her Yankee roots—something I did not fully comprehend until I bought a house not far from where she grew up in northwestern Connecticut. "I've had a pretty remarkable life," Kate once told me, recalling her childhood, "but compared to my mother and father, I'm dull." Hardly. Yet I could not recall a single conversation with Kate when she did not mention her parents and the impact they had—and continue to have—on her life. As she put it on another occasion: "The single most important thing anyone needs to know about me is that I am totally, completely the product of two damn fascinating individuals who happened to be my parents."

A new dimension was added to my sense of Kate, and much of what she had told me at long last began to come into focus. There was tangible context for Kate's stories about the colorful characters who shaped her early life in Hartford and the parents who spawned her talent, about the streets and the neighborhoods and the texture of the times in which she was raised. Kate also shared such valuable secrets as which hills offer the fastest sledding in Hartford, and how to teach my daughter the proper way to climb a birch tree (see page 132).

As she embarks on her ninth decade, Hepburn has begun to do the one thing her father told her never to do: look back. "Don't get stuck in the past," she had always quoted Dr. Thomas Hepburn as saying, "not if you want to keep moving forward, anyway."

For whatever reasons, childhood memories intensify with time. From the promontory of old age, we look back across the years and realize that—for good or ill—those figures who loomed large at the beginning cast shadows across our entire lives. Kate seems always to have known this and has never been reticent when it comes to talking about her colorful, iconoclastic parents, their offbeat brood, and the Connecticut Yankee up-bringing that endowed her with the self-esteem, the values and the fiery streak of independence (not to mention the meteoric talent) that have made her not only the greatest actress in the history of motion pictures, but also one of the world's most admired women. (Not a single poll taken in the last twenty years has failed to show Kate rating right up there in popularity alongside the president and the pope. Even teenagers young enough to be her *great*-grandchildren list her alongside idols of the moment like Madonna and Whitney Houston.) Kate has her own theories for her enduring popularity. "If you just hang around long enough," she says, "people love you for it." That is only half the answer. "I disobey rules that I happen to think are pretty silly, but I obey rules that are absolutely necessary to maintain a civilized standard of behavior. I'm like the old Flatiron Building. Maybe *it* hasn't been torn down yet, but I have a feeling I'm about to be any minute."

When I pressed Kate to cooperate with me on a book about her roots in Hartford, she suggested that I talk to her younger sister Marion, whom she more or less acknowledged to be the keeper of the Hepburn family flame. I spoke with Marion on two separate occasions in the spring of 1986, and while she felt her parents' story was one she would rather write herself, she complimented me on the magazine articles I'd written about her famous sister and willingly answered my questions. We were to talk again at a later date, but less than a month later she died—the victim of a sudden, unexpected coronary.

The death of her sister came as a jolt to Kate, a crushing personal loss. Historians and psychologists agree that one of the periods about which we are least knowledgable is the *recent* past, and Marion's death meant that another direct link with Kate's past had been broken. Marion was the second youngest of the Hepburns—nine years younger than Kate—and for me to wait any longer seemed folly.

In researching the story of the Hepburns, I soon discovered that Kate had been right all along. She is not merely acting out the role of dutiful daughter when she credits her family as the driving force behind her unparalleled achievements. Dr. Thomas and Kit Hepburn *were* "two damn fascinating individuals" who fought ferociously for what they believed in and overcame both public ridicule and soul-crushing personal tragedy to see their daughter, their "Kathy," become an American institution. Those early years shaped the life of Katharine Hepburn and, through her art and the force of her unique personality, touch our own.

Here, then, is that untold story.

—CHRISTOPHER ANDERSEN
Woodbury, Connecticut

Katharine Houghton Hepburn

1.

St. Patrick's Day, 1951

It is an unusually bleak Saturday, even for mid-March in West Hartford, Connecticut. The stately houses along Bloomfield Avenue, hidden behind a seemingly impenetrable green wall of thick vegetation during the summer months, stand naked against the late winter sky; the crusted remnants of a week-old snowstorm are piled knee-high at the roadside. None of this matters to the intense-looking man and equally intense-looking woman striding northward along the avenue, collars turned up against the bitter cold. Deep in animated conversation, clouds of white vapor billowing from their lips, they are all but oblivious to the harsh surroundings. And while the woman has long been one of the most famous people in the world, the passing townsfolk do their Yankee best to leave Katharine Hepburn and Dr. Thomas Hepburn alone.

The similarities between father and daughter are instantly evident to even the most casual observer: both are tall and solidly built (he a sturdy 5 feet 11 inches, she a lean 5 feet 8), with reddish auburn hair and freckles. Same aristocratic posture, same thoroughbred gait. Practically the same wardrobe—each wears gray flannel slacks, a cableknit sweater, an old wool coat, rubber galoshes. Off the set, Kate has not worn a dress for years, a fashion philosophy passed down from her father. "Dad never owned more than two pair of shoes at any one particular time," she would tell me years later. "The same went for suits. Only two at a time—one to wear while the other was at the cleaners."

Dr. Tom has never acquiesced to being in anyone's shadow—when introduced as Katharine Hepburn's father he is quick to point out that it is *she* who is Thomas

Hepburn's daughter. But she has always eagerly sought his advice, and he has never been reluctant to give it.

Right now, however, Dad is doing most of the listening. Kate has just wound up a grueling, ten-city tour in *As You Like It*, and she is already obsessed with her next project. She has just signed with producer Sam Spiegel to star on location in a movie version of C. S. Forester's novel *The African Queen*. James Agee has written the screenplay, John Huston will direct, and Humphrey Bogart will co-star. Lauren Bacall, "Betty" to her friends (her real name is Betty Joan Perske), will be tagging along with Bogie, Kate tells her father, but Spencer won't be there. Long separated from his wife Louise, Tracy has decided to move out of his suite at the Beverly Hills Hotel and into cozier quarters at the brick-walled Malibu guesthouse of Tracy and Hepburn's longtime friend, director George Cukor. There, sitting in his captain's chair, Tracy will pore over scripts at the big oak desk under the watchful gaze of a carved Canada goose dangling from the rafters overhead. (The wooden goose now hangs from the ceiling of Hepburn's living room in New York.)

Shooting begins in Africa next month, and in two weeks Kate will be flying alone to London for wardrobe fittings. She has always known that Tracy, a devout Catholic, will not divorce Louise, and whether or not this hurts her, she certainly isn't going to burden Dad with her problems. She does let on, however, that while the public image of Tracy and Hepburn has them locked in a constant male-female struggle for dominance in films like *Woman of the Year*, *State of the Union*, *Adam's Rib*, and *Desk Set*, when they are together it is definitely no contest. (As she once said to me, "Where change is required, *I* do the adjusting. In every relationship that exists, people have to seek a way to survive. If you really care about the person, you do what's necessary or that's the end. For the first time," she said of that point in her life, "I'd found that I really could change, and the qualities I most admired in myself I'd given up. I'd stopped being loud and bossy." Pause. "Oh, all right. I was still loud and bossy, but only behind Spencer's back.")

Independence. The freedom to come and go as one chooses, unencumbered by a relationship. Kate sees this as the ideal, and she is living it. She can look forward to her adventure in the African jungle without a trace of guilt about abandoning a husband for months. ("I wonder if men and women really suit each other. Perhaps they should live next door and just visit now and then.")

Dr. Hepburn, himself unabashedly content in his forty-seven-year marriage to Kate's mother, checks his watch, then interrupts his daughter. They are late for tea; Mother will be waiting. Kate and her passionately punctual father ("If Dad was going to pick you up and you were two minutes late, he'd leave without you") quicken the pace. Within minutes both are striding up the gravel-covered drive at 201 Bloomfield Avenue. Situated directly across the street from the campus of the University of Hartford, the three-story, twenty-four-room brick-and-stone manse sits on five wooded acres, only its three chimneys visible from the road. (Inherited by Kate and her brother following Dr. Hepburn's death in 1961, the house was donated to the University of Hartford the following year; it now serves as the res-

idence of the Paranovs—Dr. Moshe Paranov, Dean
Emeritus of the university's Hartt School of Music, and
his wife Elizabeth.)

Normally the house is full to overflowing with family
members, in-laws and assorted guests, transforming the
wide yard into a parking lot. But Kate is the only houseguest this week, although even now, at the age of forty-
three, she still thinks of this as home and of herself as
the dutiful eldest daughter. Indeed, Dr. Hepburn still
handles her finances; his secretary pays all Kate's bills
and issues her a monthly allowance check. At every
available opportunity, Kate flees to the safety of this
house with its airy, sunlit rooms, cherrywood wain-
scoting, overstuffed armchairs and burnished antiques.
Her own beige-walled room, in fact, is much the same
as it always has been. Floral print drapes still frame the
two bay windows, the maple bureau with the brass
handles still stands against the south wall, and the four-
poster is still heaped with stuffed animals. ("You see, I
never really left home. Not really.")

Kate and Dr. Hepburn waste no time hanging their
things in the hall closet. A fire in the hearth casts a warm
glow over the parlor, and Kate pauses there for a moment to warm her hands before proceeding to the dining
room. This has always been the heart of the Hepburn
household, and the image indelibly etched in Kate's
mind is of her parents sitting reading on either side of
the fireplace—Dad on the left, Mother always on the
right.

Sorry we're late, Mother. Dad and I got to talking . . .
Kate's mother has already set out—as she has every day
since the turn of the century at precisely 4 P.M.—a freshly

brewed pot of Earl Grey (a practice that has left her daughter Katharine with a lifelong disdain for teabags); the mahogany table gleams with the rattail silver service and English bone china.

But no Mother. It is only now that father and daughter realize the house is strangely, eerily quiet. Kate and Dr. Hepburn have only to look at one another in mutual silence to know that something is wrong. Together, they dash upstairs to find Katharine Houghton Hepburn— Kate's mother Kit—lying on her bed, a peaceful look on her still-handsome seventy-three-year-old face. Evidently Kit, who had suffered a small heart attack a few months earlier, felt ill and—in classic Hepburn fashion— went quietly upstairs to rest, rather than make an undignified fuss. While Dad perches on the side of the bed, searching for his wife's pulse, Kate stands there looking down at her mother with a bittersweet mixture of grief, love and anger. It was a blessing that she went so quickly, Kate will say thirty-seven years later, but *damn*. . .

2.

The Houghtons were really
something . . .

It is fitting that all of Kit Hepburn's children were given her maiden name as a middle name, for their story is as much the story of the Houghtons as of the Hepburns. In a sense this is doubly true of Katharine Hepburn, for she was her mother's namesake.

If not as famous as the Rockefellers or the Kennedys or the Vanderbilts, the Houghtons nonetheless rank as one of America's foremost dynasties, and one of the most diverse. This was the clan that founded and continues to run the Corning Glass Works, and that established the publishing house of Houghton Mifflin. Houghtons have served in Congress and as ambassadors to France, Germany, and the Court of St. James's. The family's extensive contributions to academia include Harvard University's Houghton Library, repository of one of the finest collections of rare books and manuscripts to be found anywhere. By the 1980s, the Houghtons of Corning led the family's main business into such space-age fields as fiber optics, biotechnology, and telecommunications. As a result, Katharine Houghton Hepburn and her cousins today share a family fortune estimated at nearly half a billion dollars.

As with most illustrious families, the founder of this dynasty was born in poverty, struggled to sow the seeds of empire, but died before they could bear fruit. Amory Houghton's ancestors were of Norman stock, invaders of England with William the Conqueror in 1066 who eventually settled in Lancaster, Massachusetts. Amory's great-grandfather had emigrated to New England in the 1680s, and his grandfather served with distinction during the Revolutionary War as a foot soldier in George Washington's Continental Army. His father Rufus and mother Abigail Barnard Houghton eked out a meager existence for themselves and their thirteen children on the family's hardscrabble farm in Bolton, Massachusetts.

At the age of twelve, Amory walked the four miles to nearby Lancaster to attend school, doing chores for his board and tuition. After a year he returned home, but before long he was off to Cambridge, Massachusetts, to serve as an apprentice carpenter. Eager to strike out on his own, young Amory scraped together enough money to "purchase his time" (buy out his contract) from his masters eighteen months early at the rate of eight Yankee shillings per day. Having borrowed $300, Amory launched his own business as a builder and contractor in 1833.

In her films a century later, Katharine Hepburn would thrill moviegoers and horrify directors by insisting on performing her own stunts—a streak of derring-do undoubtedly inherited in part from her great-grandfather. As Cambridge's most enthusiastic builder, Amory Houghton hoisted beams, balanced on rooftops, even worked into the night by lantern light to pay off his debt . . . while his creditors worried that Amory would be killed before he could make good on their loan. But make good he did, and by the age of twenty-three he had not only paid off his creditors but amassed a then-impressive sum of $3,000—more than enough to marry Sophronia Oakden, the handsome daughter of a local storeowner, and start a family of his own.

With an eye toward expansion, Amory rented a wharf in East Cambridge across the Charles River from Boston in 1836, and began selling coal, wood, hay, cement, lime, bark, and other commodities. For an ambitious young merchant there could be no more exciting place or time than Boston in the mid-nineteenth century, when hundreds of tall ships laden with goods from every corner of the globe crowded into the harbor. The docks were transformed into a bazaar of swirling colors and exotic scents, while Houghton and his competitors made their deals and shouted their orders over the ear-splitting din of a hundred dialects.

Over the next fifteen years the Houghton import-export business continued to prosper, but Amory, by now a thirty-seven-year-old family man and pillar of the community, grew increasingly restless. A chance encounter at a local tavern with a bluff Englishman named Gaffer Teasdale presented Amory with a challenge he could not resist. Teasdale, a veteran glass-factory manager, convinced Houghton that there was a huge potential for profit in the glass industry. Amory Houghton knew nothing about the manufacture of glass, but he was willing to gamble on Teasdale's expertise and his own merchant's instincts. In the fall of 1852, he sold out his wharf business and established the Union Glass Company at Somerville, on the outskirts of Boston. Soon the Houghton wares included bottles, lamps, and a line of pressed and molded glass for everything from window panes to lenses.

The onset of the Civil War brought with it an increased demand for bottled medical supplies, lantern globes, and glass tubing of all kinds. Filling that demand was a boon for the Union Glass Company, and now Houghton invited his eldest son, Amory Jr., to join the enterprise.

Born on October 20, 1837, Amory Jr. had been shipped off to a rigorous boarding school run by Edward Hall in

Ellington, Connecticut, and had survived to complete his high school education nearer to home in Cambridge. He then got his first taste of business by apprenticing for Lawson Valentine, soon to become one of the country's leading manufacturers of oils, paints, and varnishes.

If his father had carved a place for himself in the world of commerce through sheer grit and an innate business sense, it had been drummed into Amory Jr. that technology would be the key to success in the latter half of the nineteenth century. Determined to know all there was to know about the glass business, Amory Jr., now all of twenty, set up his own laboratory in a corner of his father's factory in Somerville. Working alone by gaslight, he conducted hundreds of experiments on the properties and composition of glass, trying every conceivable combination of ingredients to yield a product that was not only durable and light, but also beautiful.

In the spring of 1864, the elder Houghton called Amory Jr. into his office and told him of his plans to sell Union Glass Company and move to Brooklyn, New York. There, he intended to buy out and reorganize the Brooklyn Flint Glass Company, with himself and his eldest son as principal stockholders. It would turn out to be a disastrous business decision, but for the moment, at least, Amory Jr. couldn't have been more excited. Amory Jr.'s brother Charles was now old enough to join the company, and little Alfred would not be far behind. Father's expectations were high. With his sons working alongside him, the elder Houghton saw no reason why they could not make Brooklyn the glass capital of the nation.

But just four years after arriving in Brooklyn, the

———————

Houghtons faced financial ruin. The price of coal and other raw materials necessary to the manufacture of glass had turned out to be exhorbitant in New York, as was the cost of living for the Brooklyn Flint Glass employees—far higher than had been anticipated. The high wages the Houghtons were forced to pay meant there was no chance of competing with European manufacturers, whose use of indentured labor produced glass goods at substantially lower prices. Furthermore, it was only a matter of time, Katharine Hepburn's entrepreneurial forebears realized, before the new breed of labor organizers would move in on the company, forcing them to raise wages even more, cut working hours, and as a consequence lower production. The Houghtons could not afford to take the risk.

If there was any chance that the family would not have to relocate its operations, it literally went up in flames in December of 1867 when a pre-dawn fire swept through the main factory building. Snow muffled the hoofbeats of horses pulling a half-dozen ladder companies, but the clanging fire bells woke up half the borough. Father and sons watched helplessly as the blaze raged.

More than three hundred miles to the northwest, in the upstate New York town of Corning, a young inventor named Elias B. Hungerford had patented a glass venetian blind—actually a louvered shutter with narrow horizontal slats made of opaque colored glass. Hungerford approached a number of companies to manufacture his glass window blind, and while he found no takers at first in the big industrial cities of the East, he did come to learn a lot about the glass industry. Until then, Corning had been a commercial trading center—a way station for lumber (although the local forest supply was by now seriously depleted), farm products, coal, and other commodities bound for other markets. Hungerford began to see it as an ideal location for glassmaking. After all, Corning boasted a virtually limitless supply of cheap fuel, easily obtainable from the Pennsylvania coal fields just twenty miles to the south, with superb transportation by both rail and canal to the ravenous urban markets for glass to the east. If he could only convince an established manufacturer to relocate to Corning, he might succeed in pushing the town into the Industrial Revolution—and get his colored glass venetian blinds manufactured, of course.

Hungerford had heard of the Houghtons and their labor troubles in Brooklyn; he tried his mightiest to persuade the beleaguered glassmakers to move to Corning. Just how this would be managed financially was unclear at first, until in the spring of 1868 Hungerford made a remarkable offer: if the people of Corning raised $50,000 of the $125,000 needed to start a new factory, would the Houghtons pull up stakes and make Corning their base of operations? The *Corning Journal* joined Hungerford's campaign, calling upon the town in one editorial to ante up the $50,000 because "the busy hives of industry invite capital as well as labor."

On May 30, Hungerford personally handed a bank check for $50,000 to an amazed Amory Sr. Within a week, he, along with sons Amory Jr., Charles, and seventeen-year-old Alfred, had loaded their furnaces, pots, molds, and blowpipes onto canalboats for the journey up the Hudson River, through the Erie Canal, down Seneca Lake and the network of feeder canals to Corning. By the fall of 1868, the new glass factory—a T-shaped brick building constructed of nearly one million locally made bricks on a foundation of local stone—rose on a strip of land near the town's center, between the Erie Railroad and the Chemung River. Two ten-story-tall brick chimneys—one for each furnace—loomed above the plant, destined to become the foremost glassmaking center in the world.

Most of the 150 men employed at the Corning Flint Glass Works that first autumn were former workers from Brooklyn Flint who had followed the Houghtons to Corning out of loyalty—both Amorys, Sr. and Jr., were admired for their fairness and generosity—and by the promise of a hefty $3 daily wage. The arrival of the Houghtons and their workers triggered a frenzied building boom and breathed new life into the downtown business district. Hotels that not long before had been on the verge of closing, like the Corning House and the Dickenson House, were refurbished and expanded. A new hotel, the Washington, opened its doors before Thanksgiving and did a brisk holiday business.

Buoyed by the new prosperity of the post-Civil War era, Amory Jr. spearheaded the company's efforts to turn out new lines of tableware and thermometer tubing and lantern glass, confident that the boom would last. He was wrong. Within a year, the peacetime economy began its long slide toward the panic of 1873. And Corning Flint Glass, after discovering too late that the locally mined bituminous coal would not burn efficiently in its newly designed furnaces, found itself locked in a losing battle with the larger Pittsburgh glass companies for control of the lucrative Pennsylvania market.

On September 15, 1870, even as it was filling a $1,000 order from President Ulysses S. Grant for White House stemware, the Corning Flint Glass Works went into receivership. Beaten, most of his fortune sapped in the futile struggle to stave off bankruptcy, Amory Sr. retired to a farm in Westchester County. Amory Jr., Charles, and little brother Alfred were also resigned to packing their bags when word came from the plant's new owner, Boston businessman Nathan Cushing, that he wanted young Amory to take over the firm as manager—if he was up to the challenge of trying to get the company back on its feet.

At thirty-four, Amory Jr. was, like his father, a bear of a man—tall, thickly built, with a broad face, high forehead, auburn hair, and piercing blue eyes that peered from behind round, wire-rimmed spectacles. One of his more memorable features—prominent cheekbones—was shared by his now nineteen-year-old brother Alfred, who in turn would pass them on to a flamboyantly beautiful granddaughter he would never live to see.

While he had never chafed under his father's authority, young Amory did not hesitate to seize this singular opportunity to step out from Amory Sr.'s shadow and prove himself. The task before him was indeed daunting. The company's financing spigot had been virtually shut off, and the operating capital that had once flowed freely was reduced to a trickle. Straining his credit to the limit, Houghton gambled on starting up the smaller of his two furnaces. He then returned to the laboratory to invent a number of specialized items—pharmaceutical bottles, optical lenses, and the like—and these instantly found a modest but ready market.

Keeping a tight rein on the firm's operating expenses, Amory Jr. even managed to steer his company through the devastating financial panic of 1873—but not at the expense of his workers. In a move that would ensure the loyalty of a generation of Houghton employees, he insisted that the payroll be met and that all workers receive their full wage on time—even when it meant dipping into his personal accounts.

There were also family crises with which to contend. Alfred Houghton's young wife fell ill and died, leaving Amory's little brother to raise their baby daughter, one-year-old Mary, alone. Alfred had opted to set up his own firm, the Buffalo Scale Company, rather than work for the glassworks. Though by no means poverty-stricken, he had in his brief life already made enough bad financial decisions to establish himself as the poorest of the Houghton clan, and Amory Jr. breathed a sigh of relief when his little brother Alfred took beautiful, dark-haired, and thoroughly capable Caroline Garlinghouse as his second wife. Mary needed a mother, and so did Alfred. They settled in the town of West Hamburg, just south of Buffalo.

By 1875, Amory Jr. was able to buy back the plant on credit. In one of his first steps as re-owner of Corning, he set out to solve a problem that had vexed the railroad industry for years—how to make a railway signal glass that was not obscured by fog or in a storm. Although Houghton regarded himself as something of a self-taught chemist, this particular assignment was beyond his expertise. So he took a step almost unheard of among industrialists of the age—he called in a physicist from Cornell University. Three years later, the Houghtons patented a railroad signal lens with a smooth outside surface that not only pierced through dense fog and rain, but that also glowed through ice and snow, even mud. The breakthrough marked an end to Corning Glass's long struggle for survival.

3.

. . . and Mother was a Houghton

Amory Jr.'s faith in the company his father founded had at last been vindicated, and it meant millions in profits for the family. By way of rewarding himself, Houghton cast about for a new home—one befitting a captain of industry. Shortly after New Year's, 1878, he paid $10,000 for an imposing neo-Gothic stone manor occupying an entire city block between Cedar and Pine streets on Third Street. Ringed by a wrought-iron fence, this had been the residence of Corning's leading banker, George W. Patterson—until Patterson's bank failed and he was sent to Auburn prison for fraud.

Amory, the most righteous of businessmen in this bare-knuckled age of wheeler-dealers and high-stakes con men, had no worries about joining Patterson in jail or in the poorhouse, whether on his own account or due to the dereliction of others. It was no accident that from his new hillside vantage point just a few blocks away from the bustling glassworks he could keep a watchful eye on his empire. With Houghton's arrival, the town's most socially ambitious families began moving into the neighborhood, transforming the once-park-like natural setting into an architectural hodgepodge of periods and styles. Houses of every conceivable design sprang up around Third Street—gingerbread Victorians with peaked gables and broad wraparound porches, pillared and porticoed antebellum mansions, dour brick Georgians, the occasional white clapboard captain's house topped by a widow's walk, even mansard-roofed chateaux. But almost by design, lest anyone offend Corning's leading citizen, none was quite as imposing as the Houghton estate. (The residence was eventually donated to the Corning Academy. The house itself was razed in 1920 and a new academy constructed on the site.) Amory took up residence on February 2, 1878—a date also significant for the arrival of the newest Houghton—Alfred and Caroline's daughter Katharine.

"Kit," as she was known even before she could walk, maintained her monopoly on her parents' attention for only a short time; she was followed in rapid succession by Edith, born in 1879, and Marion, who arrived in 1884. All three girls were strikingly attractive, but a quality valued even more by their mother was their intelligence. Caroline, an exceptionally bright young woman who nonetheless had been forbidden by her father to attend college, had already ruffled feathers in the town by conducting one of New York State's first social discussion clubs in her own parlor. These informal gatherings—held in the afternoons, since women of the time were generally discouraged from venturing unescorted from their own homes after dark—were conducted in the radical belief that women should be apprised of current affairs, and that in some rare instances they might even have some intelligent observations to offer concerning the significant events of the day.

While Caroline Houghton and the other more daring women of Buffalo discussed such pressing social issues as the temperance movement and the Russo-Turkish War, a news story that would literally electrify the nation was unfolding virtually on their doorstep. In September of 1879, Kit's Uncle Amory received an unusual order from a fellow named T. A. Edison. It seemed that this Edison was some sort of inventor and that he claimed to be on the verge of perfecting the first practical incandescent lamp. His sole remaining obstacle was to find a globe that would hold the vacuum required to sustain the glow of a filament. Edison had assigned glassblower Ludwig Boehm to create the pear-shaped bulb Edison envisioned, but Boehm's experiments had proved fruitless and had exhausted his supplies of glass. In desperation, Thomas Alva Edison turned to Corning.

"Dear Sir," replied Houghton, "We cannot fill your order for we only make lead glass." Leaded glass, he pointed out, could not be made to seal properly with Edison's platinum lead-in wires. Edison's research stalled for another six months until a Pennsylvania glassblower bound for Corning to pick up tubing came across an article on Edison's dilemma while waiting for a train. William Holzer wrote to Edison asking to be hired, and he was.

Holzer argued that despite Amory's first response to Edison, only the Houghtons of Corning and their army of experts were equipped to solve the problem, and in the summer of 1879 Edison dispatched one of his own assistants to Corning. The assistant worked feverishly with Corning's most skilled gaffers but to no avail, though Corning's glass seemed less a problem than fabricating the right shape. He was about to give up and return empty-handed to Edison's headquarters in Menlo Park, New Jersey, when out of the corner of his eye he spotted a bored apprentice entertaining himself with a glob of molten glass on the end of a glass-blowing pipe. Tossing his head back and tilting the pipe skyward as if he were about to hit a high note on an imaginary clarinet, the young man blithely blew a small, elegant glass bubble. Edison's assistant cabled his boss that he—or rather, the shop boy—had stumbled upon the perfect shape for the electric light bulb. (Eventually, three men stepped forward to take credit for being the boy with the bubble: Frederick Beuerlein, Joseph Baxter, and James Goggin.)

On November 17, 1880, 307 of the bulbs were sent to Menlo Park. The following year, William Holzer, the man responsible for marrying the talents of Edison and Houghton, made a love match of his own: he married Edison's sister. For Corning Glass, meantime, Edison had switched on an entire new product line that soon accounted for well over a third of the company's total sales, beginning the Houghton family's century-long reign as the world's leading manufacturer of light bulbs.

Even this grandest of Amory's exploits failed to impress his nieces. Nor did the opulent trappings of his power and status. Their father Alfred's original success with his own company enabled them to live comfortably enough—they could afford a nanny as well as a maid—though hardly on so grand a scale as the rest of the Houghton clan. And while folks in Corning snapped to attention at the mere mention of the family name, Kit and her sisters (older half-sister Mary was now away at school) were by no means looked upon as royalty in West Hamburg. Still, Caroline saw to it that no expense was spared when it came to her girls' education. They were close enough in age to be tutored at home together, and all three—particularly Edith—inherited their mother's seemingly unquenchable thirst for knowledge. They were equally intent on having their fair share of fun. That meant bobsledding, skating, and fierce snowball fights during Buffalo's famous winters, swimming and sailing on Lake Erie during the humid summer months, bicycling and lawn games in between. The girls were also willing participants in the fads of the time, like the rage for stringing buttons. The local newspaper in Corning ran a feature on one twelve-year-old who had strung 2,296 buttons to a length of 31 feet—each button, the paper marveled, "having a loop-eye, and no two alike."

Kit's idyllic world started to crumble in the autumn of 1892 when her mother suddenly fell ill and was rushed to the hospital. Caroline appeared to recover, but over the next few months Kit noticed that her mother's health seemed to be deteriorating.

One chilly October evening Caroline felt strong enough to go out for a brisk stroll with her daughters along West Hamburg's leaf-strewn streets. Edith and Marion may have been preoccupied with jumping into leaf piles they spotted along the way, but Kit listened intently as her mother told her once again how essential it was for all people—including women—to get a top-notch education, and of the dream she had that her girls would someday attend what she was convinced was the finest women's college of all, Bryn Mawr.

A palpable sense of dread permeated the Alfred Houghton household, though it is highly doubtful that even Kit, the most sensitive of the children, fully comprehended the gravity of the situation. Her father had taken the doctor's diagnosis of Caroline's cancer hard; it seemed nothing short of incredible to him that at the age of forty-one he should have to endure watching a second wife's slow, painful death. But the Houghtons had always been a stolid Yankee lot—certainly not the sort given to outward displays of emotion—and he was not about to shed any unmanly tears, certainly not in front of members of his own family. Instead, he handled the crisis the only way he knew, by immersing himself even deeper in his work.

In mid-October, Alfred Houghton collapsed from nervous exhaustion. Rather than be an added burden to Caroline and the children, he accepted his oldest brother Amory's invitation to recuperate at the Houghton mansion on Third Street. Amory personally escorted Alfred to Corning, where he remained under doctor's strict orders to do nothing but rest. After two weeks, looking more relaxed and fit than he had in months, Alfred told Amory he was going off by himself for an evening carriage ride. He did not return.

Search parties were dispatched and, according to the *Corning Weekly Journal*, "scoured the city and vicinity during the night." Yet it was a Fall Brook, New York railroad man named Ira Miller who made the grisly discovery shortly after dawn while helping to run a boxcar through Walker's lumberyard to Denison's warehouse. The lumberyard, Corning's busiest, was located not far from the glassworks, just northeast of the post office and west of the Chemung River. As the boxcar rolled through the lumberyard, Miller spotted Alfred Houghton sprawled face-up on a pile of two-by-fours. Miller approached and was horrified to discover blood coming from a pistol shot through Alfred's temple. A revolver was still clenched in the dead man's right hand.

Kit, if only for the sake of her younger sisters, had kept up a brave front in the face of their mother's illness, even after being told it was terminal. Yet nothing could have prepared her for the morning of October 29, 1892, when a telegram arrived saying that her father had been found, an apparent suicide. The body, the telegram continued, had been taken to Fletcher & Cook's undertaking establishment pending instructions from the family of the deceased, which Amory promptly furnished.

The Lackawanna express train carrying the remains of Alfred Augustus Houghton left Corning at 5:03 that afternoon bound for Buffalo. Caroline was too ill to attend her husband's funeral, but Kit insisted that she and her sisters go. Amory Houghton was impressed with the dignified way in which his nieces conducted themselves.

Probably out of deference to Corning's first family, the papers handled Alfred's suicide with considerable restraint. Under the discreet headline *A Sad Death*, the *Corning Daily Democrat* reported that "the people of this city were greatly shocked this morning at the announcement of the death of Alfred Augustus Houghton," who had been "a sufferer of nervous prostration." He had come to visit his brother, the *Democrat* continued, in hopes that "absolute relief from business cares would soon restore him to health. Almost the entire management of the Buffalo Scale Works has been in Mr. Houghton's hands," the article continued, "and it proved too great a strain for him. His untimely death will be greatly mourned."

The *Corning Weekly Journal* eulogized Alfred Houghton even more effusively in its piece five days later: "He had a beautiful home at West Hamburg, near Buffalo, where he leaves a wife and four children. He was a man of uncommon business ability, and of spotless integrity. His death in the prime of his manhood and his usefulness causes oppressive sorrow.''

In Buffalo, Alfred's rather spectacular suicide might have been expected to make the front page; he was, after all, not only one of the city's most prominent business leaders, but he was also a Houghton. Instead, only one of the local papers carried the story at all—a terse account under the headline *A.A. HOUGHTON SHOOTS HIM-SELF—One of the Owners of the Buffalo Scale Works Kills Himself in a Fit of Despondency.*

Kit might easily have viewed her father's suicide as an act of unforgivable selfishness. By taking his own life, he had insured that his young daughters would be parentless. But there was no time for self-pity.

Five days after her father's death, Kit knelt at her mother's bedside. Grasping her eldest daughter's hand, Caroline told Kit that she and the girls would now be taken care of by Uncle Amory. ''Get an education,'' she whispered to Kit. ''I want you to go to Bryn Mawr, and then I want you to make sure that Edith and Marion go there too. *You must all get an education.* You'll have some money, but not as much as the rest of the family. Don't be drowned by the rich relatives. Keep your independence. Be your own person, and never, never be afraid of anything.'' Moments later, Caroline Garlinghouse Houghton was dead at the age of thirty-three. And, at fourteen, Kit was an orphan.

4.

Going to live with Uncle Amory,
her mother's last words stuck
with her. She really wanted to
amount to something.

As the 8:15 for Corning pulled out of Buffalo station with Kit and her sisters aboard, the new wards of Amory Houghton wondered what it would be like living in that cavernous, impersonal house on the hill. Uncle Amory had always seemed distant and somewhat imperious— a benevolent, perhaps even loving, patriarch, but one certainly accustomed to getting his own way.

Those closest to him, insofar as he allowed anyone to get close to him, noticed that Amory Houghton had indeed grown increasingly cold and unsympathetic—the inevitable result of waging the nineteenth-century industrialist's apparently unending war against unionization. Corning Glass, a company that hired young boys to learn the glassworker's trade, then made them labor under conditions that could only be described as Dickensian, was an obvious target for organizers of the day. Sweat poured off the glassblowers and their grit-covered helpers as they toiled eleven hours at a stretch, spending much of that time directly in front of the furnaces hammering, rolling, and shaping molten glass into such incongruously genteel items as goblets, vases, candlesticks, and fishbowls. Tempers soared with the temperatures, and fights among workers were commonplace. But the pay was generous—as high as $5 per day—and if Houghton was forced by a union to cut his workers' productivity, the European glass factories with their cheap labor would surely step in to fill the void.

By 1891 the American Flint Glass Workers Union had secured enough of a toehold in Corning to establish a local there and to organize a walkout. Houghton viewed the strike as a betrayal; after all, it was he who had been making sure the workers always got their pay, even in the dark days when the company was struggling back from bankruptcy. With antiunion sentiment running high in the community, and with the local press behind him, Houghton responded to the walkout with a lockout of his own. Many of the strikers returned to their jobs immediately; those who chose to stick with the union were merely replaced.

Tensions ran high for the next several months, climaxing on a foggy night at a railroad crossing outside the tiny hamlet of Ravenna, Ohio. Shortly before three in the morning, a train carrying striking Corning workers returning home for a summer holiday collided with a freight carrying livestock, and seventeen men died. In a tragically ironic twist, the railroad had failed to install one of Houghton's lifesaving Corning Glass signals at the deadly intersection.

The incident at Ravenna would be shamelessly exploited by labor; the union would go so far as to hold its national convention in Corning, complete with memorial service, parade, and ceremonial unveiling of a monument dedicated to the victims. Houghton managed to fend off any personal criticism, in part by stepping up his philanthropic efforts. The strategy worked: six months after the Ravenna catastrophe, he was unanimously elected president of the Corning School Board. "Although engrossed in business affairs," the *Corning Leader* would later editorialize, "he was no figurehead on the board of education but was its mainspring and directing genius, giving much time and thought to the problems of school growth and being a steady advocate of progress in school affairs. His long and valuable services on the board of education attest to his public spirit and his deep interest in the cause of education."

That "deep interest" did not extend to higher education for his nieces, however. Like most of his fellow Americans, he thought the very idea ludicrous. Why waste the resources of America's colleges and universities on women who would likely never vote and never hold a job, he reasoned. The twentieth-century woman should, like the generations that preceded her, be content to live out her life as wife and homemaker. Those few hapless souls who did choose a college degree over more natural feminine pursuits were, Houghton firmly believed, doomed to become bitter spinsters.

Houghton had practically built the American glass industry singlehandedly and in 1894 he vanquished the unions when Local 108 folded altogether. (The American Flint Glass Union would not succeed in reorganizing Corning's workers until 1943.) Kit was another matter. No sooner had she landed on Amory Houghton's doorstep than the feisty young lady informed her uncle of her mother's wish that all three of her daughters attend Bryn Mawr. Out of the question, Uncle Amory declared. Undaunted, Kit enlisted the support of Uncle Amory's own young sons Alanson and Arthur, but even that proved unavailing. Uncle Amory brusquely informed the girls that, once and for all, they would *not* be attending Bryn Mawr—or any other college, for that matter. Out of respect for their mother's wishes, however, they would be permitted to attend one of the more reputable finishing schools. Miss Hewitt's in New York City, perhaps, or Miss Porter's in Farmington, Connecticut.

Kit was not about to give up. "All three girls viewed their mother's last wish as sacrosanct," Kit's own actress daughter would say years later. "It was more of a command than a wish, and they were headstrong enough to stand up to their uncle and win."

But how? The Houghton girls soon became a familiar sight strolling the hilly streets of Corning, talking among themselves. One local girl from a working class family was particularly given to watching Kit, Edith, and Marion, albeit from a safe distance. Little Maggie Higgins, who would eventually become one of Kit's closest allies in the birth-control movement, could not have guessed that the rich Houghton girls were plotting to thwart their Uncle Amory. Years later, Maggie Higgins would herself be making headlines under her married name: Margaret Sanger.

Before they could devise a workable plan, however, the girls were packed off to stay with relatives in Canandaigua, a sleepy resort town in New York's Finger Lakes region. There they would be out of harm's way—and out of Uncle Amory's graying hair while he mulled the weighty question of which finishing school would be suitable for his brother's three daughters.

Kit was not about to give up on Mother's dream. "Uncle can run a big factory," she told her sisters, "but he can't run me." Besides, there was more at stake than just Kit's future. Edith in particular had shown a keen interest in science, and if Uncle Amory succeeded in squelching Kit's college plans, Edith or Marion stood even less chance of ever entering the halls of academe.

Their country cousins instantly proved themselves to be warm, caring hosts, and the setting on the shores of

---

51

shimmering Lake Canandaigua seemed idyllic. All of which made Kit's decision that much more difficult. "We love Uncle very much," she told Edith and Marion, "but there's no point in letting him alter the course of our lives. The first step is to make our relatives not want us."

With that, Kit embarked on a campaign to drive her cousins crazy enough to kick the three of them out. The parlor was situated directly beneath the girls' room, so every evening after she and her her sisters had gone to bed, Kit watched at the door while Edith and Marion got down on hands and knees and began thumping on the floor. Their hosts, wondering about the commotion, would then bound up the stairs to find three young girls sitting primly in their room, listening as Kit read to them. Once the girls were satisfied their hosts had returned to the comfort of the parlor and begun to settle in, they resumed their noisy antics.

The ritual, which would last about an hour each night, went on for two full weeks—the country cousins had more stamina than Kit had anticipated (no doubt spurred by their desire not to offend powerful Amory)—before a meeting was hastily called to decide what to do with the noisy guests. Desperate, the nervewracked country cousins wired Houghton that his frisky wards were too much to handle; they would be on the next train to Corning.

One afternoon, with the girls back at the mansion, Amory was gazing out his library window at the smoke billowing from his factory's ten brick chimneys as his attorney explained the delicate situation to him.

Crouched outside the library door was Kit, eavesdropping. In a provision of his will that indicated Kit's father was every bit as farsighted and enlightened as his wife, Alfred Houghton had stipulated that his elder brother Amory be appointed temporary guardian only. It was up to the girls themselves to choose their permanent guardian. "That meant," Kit's daughter (and Kate's younger sister) Marion would explain ninety years later, "that he believed in the revolutionary idea of women— even women as young as Mother was then, just four- teen—having a right to make their own decisions about their own lives."

Kit's ears were burning. There was more. Now, the lawyer continued, the court would in all likelihood ask Kit, being the eldest, to name their permanent guardian. Just a formality, he reassured his worried client. Amory Houghton would then of course be appointed, clearing the way for him to dispatch them to a proper finishing school straightaway.

The day in court arrived, and the white-maned, bes- pectacled judge asked Kit to name her preference as permanent guardian. The entire courtroom—not to mention Uncle Amory—sat in stunned silence as Kit stood up and instead named Cousin Alanson's good- looking lawyer friend, who just happened to be slouch- ing in the back of the courtroom. The fellow, a notorious ladies' man who boasted credentials as a leading cru- sader for women's education, told the confused judge that he would be delighted to serve as the girls' guard- ian. Uncle Amory's attorney protested, but the court saw no reason to deny Kit's request; she was clearly an articulate, intelligent young woman, and according to her father's last will and testament she was acting well within her rights to select whomever she pleased.

Left without any other alternative, Uncle Amory relented. His gruff exterior, it turned out, belied a genuine affection and abiding concern for his nieces; besides, he was not about to hand their futures over to a radical-thinking ne'er-do-well. In exchange for being appointed her permanent guardian, Amory would permit Kit, and then her sisters, to attend college.

Kit savored her first political triumph. She was not yet fifteen, and yet, through a series of brilliant manuevers, she had managed to outfox one of America's most cunning captains of industry on his home ground.

Or had she? Uncle Amory knew all too well that applying for admission to a prestigious institution of higher learning was not the same as being accepted. None of the girls had ever actually attended a school, and the sort of upper-class tutoring they had received up until now was designed to prepare them for marriage, motherhood, and a life in society. They were, in short, capable of functioning effortlessly at a tea party, but ill-equipped to pass the college boards.

Uncle Amory sat back smugly and waited for Kit to fail. Kit knew he was counting on it, but she was still in the game to win. Without bothering to enlist Uncle Amory's help (it is doubtful he would have willingly given it at that stage), Kit dashed off a letter to the Bryn Mawr admissions office asking for its entrance requirements. Once she had a rundown of required subjects in hand, as well as a detailed description of the college's entrance examination, she asked the college to recommend tutors in the Corning area. Kit then screened the candidates before hiring the necessary tutors for herself and her sisters. The cost of the tutors, she insisted to Uncle Amory, was to be paid out of their inheritance.

With characteristic zeal, Kit plunged into her studies. It heralded the beginning of a lifelong love of books and ideas but, typically, only those books and ideas that she found intriguing. Mathematics and the sciences she found trying at best. In fact, there was a yawning gap between being an eager student of life and a grade-seeking, teacher-pleasing pupil.

Shortly after her sixteenth birthday, Kit announced to Uncle Amory that she was ready—well, as ready as she could ever be—to take the entrance examinations. When she had surprised him in the courtroom two years earlier, Kit had abruptly seized her uncle's attention. Now this gutsy young girl was earning his respect.

The day she was to journey down to Bryn Mawr, Kit was flabbergasted when Uncle Amory boarded the train for Philadelphia with her. Once there, he escorted her to a luxurious hotel suite where they would both stay in comfort during the two grueling days of exams. Kit passed—barely—and found herself enrolled in the Bryn Mawr freshman class of 1895. Her mother's dream was on the brink of being realized, and no one was prouder than Uncle Amory that Kit was a Houghton of Corning.

5.

They said Mother had the
longest neck, the tightest collar,
and the smallest waist
of anyone at Bryn Mawr.

Bryn Mawr was less than a decade old when Kit Houghton arrived there in the fall of 1895. Yet of the Seven
Sister colleges (Mount Holyoke, Vassar, Wellesley,
Smith, Radcliffe, and Barnard were the others) it had an
undeniable free-spirited style all its own. Not, however,
at the expense of scholastic excellence. Bryn Mawr was
the first women's college to offer a Ph.D., and its first
faculty included a young professor of history and politics
named Woodrow Wilson.

Bryn Mawr was founded by wealthy Quaker physician
Joseph Wright Taylor as "a place for the advanced education of our young female Friends, affording them all
the advantages of a college education which are so freely
offered to young men." It took a bold, unstoppable
young visionary named M. Carey Thomas to turn Taylor's dream into reality.

"Mother was influenced greatly by Carey Thomas,"
Kate would tell me. "All the women of her generation
idolized her. And they were right to." In her younger
days, Carey Thomas was very much like Kit Houghton.
Fresh from earning her Ph.D. *summa cum laude* from Zu-
rich, Thomas wrote a letter to the Bryn Mawr board of
trustees urging them to hire her as the college's first
president. The trustees instead appointed one of their
own to the position of president, James E. Rhoads, but
they did hire Carey Thomas as Bryn Mawr's first dean.

Then, and later as president, Thomas set out to make
Bryn Mawr the equal of men's universities at the time.
The entrance requirements were as stringent as any set
by Harvard or Yale (Kit had had a particularly rough
time with Greek), and the curriculum at Bryn Mawr
made no concessions to traditional "female" subjects

such as domestic science. Students were required to wear on campus what heretofore had been regarded the traditional uniform of male collegians: the cap and gown.

To promote a sense of self-esteem and independence, students were accorded an unusual degree of privacy under conditions that would today seem almost sybaritic. Every undergraduate had at the very least one private room, and maidservice (students did not even have to make their own beds) was included in the cost. A single room—the minimum—cost $100 per year; a two-room suite with sitting room went for $350. Kit Houghton's two-bedroom suite was comfortably furnished with bookcases, armchairs, and study tables heaped with leatherbound texts. Kit settled in with framed family photographs crowding the marble mantlepiece in the sitting room, porcelain vases brimming with flowers, and oriental carpets covering the floors.

Here Kit carried on her mother's practice of presiding over a discussion group. There was no shortage of eager participants. Not only was her fifteen-inch waist the smallest at Bryn Mawr, but the mannish ties and oversized black satin bows worn behind her upswept Gibson Girl hairdo were the largest. Overnight, Kit was a bona fide campus star, and she was all too aware of it.

Kit soon proved herself to be one of the most high-spirited students at a high-spirited school. Uncle Amory and the rest of the Houghtons were accomplished equestrians, and Kit was no exception. At Bryn Mawr, she and her friends scandalized the locals not only by galloping straight down Main Street, but by doing it astride and not sidesaddle, the only socially acceptable way for a lady to ride horseback in the 1890s.

Another favorite pastime for Kit and her cohorts was to crouch behind tombstones in a nearby family cemetery and sneak a smoke. In this they were very much abreast of the times, for cigarette smoking had become one of the most hotly debated issues not only at Bryn Mawr, but on campuses across the country. It was an issue not because of the possible health hazards—virtually unknown at the time—but because cigarette smoking in defiance of rigid social convention symbolized a young woman's sexual awakening. The well-heeled daughters of America's finest families, sent away from home to spend nearly all their hours both waking and sleeping in the company of other women, could hardly be expected to pass up the chance to declare themselves women of the world merely by lighting up.

Carey Thomas found herself in an awkward situation. On the one hand, she had set out singlehandedly to mold an institution by, for, and of women—and was well on the road to realizing that goal. But the fact remained that Thomas was running a Quaker institution and answered to a Quaker board of trustees; in order to remain at the helm of Bryn Mawr, she had to declare her adherence to Quaker beliefs—and inevitably this included a strong opposition to smoking. For Thomas, who had done her own share of closet smoking as an undergraduate at Cornell University, these declarations were at best politically expedient: After her retirement from Bryn Mawr in 1922, she returned to cigarettes—and became an Episcopalian.

As president of the college, however, she had a mini-rebellion on her hands, and its ringleader was Kit Houghton. Expulsion would have been the simplest solution and one, it might have been argued, that Kit justified by her flagrant misconduct. But President Thomas—"P.T." to her adoring students—had two compelling reasons not to throw Kit out of school. First, the college stood to benefit handsomely from Amory Houghton's largesse and, equally important, spunky Kit Houghton reminded her of herself at that age. (As an adolescent, Thomas had been so impatient and hot-headed as to have earned the nickname of "Rush"). Every morning at 8:45, the entire student body gathered in the assembly hall to hear Thomas urge each one to believe in herself and to believe in women. Young Miss Houghton, for all her outwardly rambunctious behavior, already clearly believed in both.

One afternoon during her sophomore year, Kit was summoned to the president's office. She fully expected the worst. She had allowed her grades to slide and had made something of a spectacle of herself. Carey Thomas would have no choice but to discipline her—perhaps even expel her. But instead of playing the stern administrator, Thomas smiled warmly and gently explained to Kit why she was being asked to change her ways. Thomas and her contemporaries had fought hard to establish a women's college of Bryn Mawr's caliber, and now Kit was behaving as if she had nothing but contempt for the opportunities being offered her. Her antics—particularly her penchant for smoking behind tombstones—and those of her followers were sabotaging the school's good name, not to mention the cause of higher education for women in general.

Thomas's tactics worked. Kit was appalled that she could have been so arrogant, so blind to the damage she was causing. She promptly gave up smoking behind tombstones and concentrated on her studies for a degree in art. She continued to hold forth at her parlor discussion groups (now joined by her sister Edith, an incoming freshman whose own study habits were nothing short of exemplary), even while her knowledge in the area of foreign affairs remained severely wanting. When, on February 16, 1898, one of her classmates rushed into the dormitory waving the headline MAINE SUNK, Kit was nonplussed. "How could Maine sink?" she asked. "Was there an earthquake?" (Thomas laughed when word of Kit's remark reached her, undoubtedly at least in part out of self-recognition; despite the president's undeniable intellectual brilliance, her own shortcomings included a legendary inability to spell.)

Still, Kit's grades improved markedly, and she even joined in a few extracurricular activities. In her junior year, she also took to the playing fields in earnest. A natural athlete at 5 feet 8 inches in her stocking feet, she quickly became a star at basketball despite being required to wear the customary player's dress of velvet so long and heavy that it brushed the tops of her highbutton shoes.

As part of her involvement in student affairs, Kit for the first time tested herself as a public speaker. Spelling may not have been Carey Thomas's strong suit, but she cared very much how her students *sounded*. Kit's clipped Yankee accent and the high-pitched, crackling timbre of her voice would eventually become a Hepburn trademark—irritating to some, charming to others, and always unforgettable.

Kit Houghton campaigned for treasurer of the student

Self-Governance Association and won handily—this despite the sobering fact that her financial acumen was nil. "Mother did have an enormous curiousity about the world," Kate says, "but she knew absolutely nothing about money."

From the very beginning, Kit spent far beyond her generous allowance. When her fervent pleas to Uncle Amory for more money went unheeded, she took action. In a move to supplement her income that her uncle would have found shocking, had she thought to tell him, Kit posted a notice in the dormitory washroom offering to tutor "anyone on any subject." The tutoring sessions proved lucrative enough, but Kit now found little time for her own studies. In her senior year she hardly cracked a book until the night before a test. She got away handsomely with such eleventh-hour cramming, sailing through every one of her final exams, and wound up graduating near the top of her class.

Poised on the brink of their new lives and of a new century, the fresh-faced members of the Bryn Mawr Class of '99 were asked by yearbook editors to list their postgraduate goals. Most spoke breathlessly of the large families they would raise and the brilliant careers the future held in store for them. Kit had only one goal in mind: "To raise Hell with established customs."

6.

My mother was confronted
with the decision that faced
a lot of women—family or
career. But first she wanted
to see a little of the world.

September, 1899. The Treaty of Paris had just been ratified by the United States Senate, ending the Spanish-
American War. The Boer War was raging in South Africa, China was on the brink of the Boxer Rebellion, and
in Vienna an unknown doctor named Sigmund Freud
was finishing his landmark work, *The Interpretation of
Dreams*.

It was also the year Kit Houghton journeyed north to
Boston and enrolled as a graduate student at Harvard,
or at least the closest thing to Harvard for a young woman at the turn of the century: Radcliffe.

If Bryn Mawr was the most scholastically challenging
of the women's colleges, by 1899 it was facing stiff competition from Radcliffe. Drawing as it did on Harvard's
then-unequaled faculty, Radcliffe was particularly strong
in the arts and thus a natural next stop in Kit's determined education. She thrilled to the thought of learning
at the feet of the greatest professors in the country. But
her reasons for seeking her master's degree in art from
Radcliffe were not entirely academic. For all her headstrong misbehavior, Kit had led a comparatively cloistered life at Bryn Mawr, and the prospect of living and
studying in cultured, cosmopolitan, *exciting* Boston was
enormously attractive. Kit felt an almost spiritual connection with the city, but this was to be expected. After
all, the Houghton family's roots were firmly planted in
Massachusetts soil. Away from class, Kit watched Harvard men rowing on the Charles (and was watched in
return), roamed the antiquity-filled galleries of the Museum of Fine Arts, and listened avidly as would-be Patrick Henrys literally climbed onto soapboxes in Boston

Common to debate everything from Darwin to the gold standard.

Kit earned her master's degree in June of 1900, but had no intention of immediately returning home. For months, she and her best friend Mary Towle had planned to reward themselves with a European holiday. Once again, of course, Kit was strapped for funds. The next installment of her allowance was not due for another six months, so she would have to pry an advance out of her flinty Uncle Amory. She started off by reminding him that he had not hesitated to send his own son Alanson off to Paris for his postgraduate studies at the Sorbonne, and followed by arguing that no art student's education could truly be complete without a pilgrimage to the art center of the world.

True to form, Uncle Amory would not be budged. Equally true to form, Kit managed to scrape together enough money for passage to Cherbourg and set sail in October with just ten dollars in her purse. Ten days later, with tickets for the boat train purchased from Mary Towle's own less-than-ample funds, Kit and her friend arrived in the Paris of Pissarro, Monet, Degas and Rodin, of Zola and Jules Verne, of Toulouse-Lautrec and the Moulin Rouge.

Their first challenge was to find a place to stay. Kit donned her best satin dress and her mother's pearls, then convinced a bistro owner near the Gare du Nord to rent them one of the rooms above his run-down establishment. She had no money now, she told him in her quite fluent Bryn Mawr French, but soon she would, once her rich uncle came through with her allowance.

The bistro owner saw no reason to doubt Kit's story; she looked and sounded every inch the self-assured rich American.

Now broke, Kit and Mary spent hours at the Louvre and at Napoleon's Tomb, strolling through the Bois de Boulogne and frequenting musty cathedrals. And each day at dusk they returned to the bistro to order up their only meal and dine in their cramped room. At the advice of the bistro owner, they did not venture downstairs after dark. At first Kit doubted that there was any real danger—until she was awakened one night by the sound of a commotion downstairs. When she and Mary tiptoed to the top of the stairs to investigate, they saw a body sprawled on the floor in a pool of blood and one of the bistro's rougher-looking customers being taken into custody by several baton-wielding *gendarmes*. It seemed, the bistro owner tried to explain to his American guests, that one man had stabbed another to death in a fight over a woman. Though now appreciating the owner's earlier advice, Kit did not react with alarm. The gruesome crime of passion she had almost witnessed could be chalked up as merely another colorful quirk of the Parisian working class.

Just after New Year's Day, 1901, Kit's allowance from Uncle Amory—plus a generous bonus—arrived at last. The Houghton family patriarch had, as his niece suspected, felt guilty for letting his innocent young charge travel to Europe practically penniless.

Kit settled accounts with the bistro owner, but rather than head straight home as they had originally planned, the two young women used the windfall from Uncle Amory to make a little sidetrip—to Monte Carlo.

Even after the breathtaking beauty of Paris, Kit could not help but be struck by the surreal splendor of Monaco. During the day, a pink-walled sixteenth-century fairytale palace shimmered in the sun while teak-hulled yachts bobbed lazily in the harbor below. After nightfall, Monaco's heart, the Monte Carlo casino, became an irresistible spectacle. Beneath glittering Baccarat chandeliers, Europe's idle rich came to stake small fortunes on a roll of the dice or a hand of *chemin de fer*. Kit stayed, watched, and spent.

Once again Kit found herself down to her last few dollars, and once again she staked all on a hunch. Having been content for a time merely to observe the high-stakes action, the striking young American with the fifteen-inch waist and the upswept auburn hair proceeded to the roulette table, where after just a few spins of the wheel she parlayed the meager remains of Uncle Amory's conscience money into a handsome $200—more than enough for the girls' return passage to New York.

Aboard ship, Kit felt more assured than ever, the last vestige of the awkward schoolgirl gone. Now she was the worldly sophisticate, able to move confidently among the other passengers, even to return a few of the many admiring male glances that inevitably came her way. Having attained her maturity in a world of women, Kit found herself, somewhat to her surprise, altogether comfortable in the company of men.

During the passage home, Kit weighed her options for the future. She had fulfilled her mother's dying wish that she get the best possible education, but now what? Mother had wisely left the rest up to her. By now Kit had an insatiable curiosity about—and strong opinions concerning—art and sex and politics and . . . everything. Her brief stint as a tutor back at Bryn Mawr had proved that she could teach. Perhaps that should be her career.

By the time the Statute of Liberty, not yet turned green by decades of oxidation, appeared like a slightly tarnished penny on the horizon, she had made up her mind. What she craved most was the only thing she had been denied from an early age—the kind of close and caring family life that had ended with the tragic deaths of her parents. Astonishingly, the career that most appealed to Kit now required neither a bachelor's degree from Bryn Mawr or a master's from Radcliffe. After careful deliberation, she decided that her life's work would be that of wife and mother.

7.

Mother took one look at him and said, "Boy, that's for me!"

At the turn of the century, women did not pursue men, at least not in theory. A man, as the saying went, chased a woman until she caught him. For the purpose of looking over a multitude of eligible—and affluent—bachelors, one of the most ideal locations in America was Baltimore and its Johns Hopkins University, where Kit's sister Edith just happened to be in her second year of medical school. (At the time, Johns Hopkins was the only medical school in the country to accept female students, thanks largely to a wealthy and anonymous benefactress who made that a condition for her largesse.) Still, the worldly-wise Kit was not entirely certain that she suited a provincial town like Baltimore, or vice versa.

It took an exhibition fencing match to change her mind. While visiting her sister in the spring of 1901, Kit went along to watch Edith, an amateur fencer, thrust and parry with a tall, broad-shouldered third-year student from Virginia. Edith was a superb fencer, but Kit barely noticed; she was dazzled by her sister's husky, redheaded opponent. His name was Tom Hepburn, and he was the son of an impoverished but pedigreed Episcopal minister. After perfunctory introductions, he rushed off to catch his next class. Kit waited until he was out of earshot to nudge Edith. "Boy," she sighed, "that's for me! He's the most beautiful creature I've ever seen." Edith hastened to note that the object of her desire didn't have "one red cent" to his name, and that Kit hadn't struggled against the odds this long to throw away her future on a penniless medical student.

Kit would have none of it. It was the present, not the future, that concerned her. "I'd marry him even if it meant I'd die in a year—*and* go to hell!"

Kit promptly moved into Edith's apartment ("Mother was determined to get to know this Hepburn fellow") and took a job teaching at Baltimore's exclusive Calvert School. As a teacher, Kit employed the same eleventh-hour techniques she had used so successfully as a student at Bryn Mawr. "She could teach a subject she knew absolutely nothing about," Kate recalls with pride, "by keeping one day ahead of the class. They never caught on."

The relationship with young Tom Hepburn did. As luck would have it, Johns Hopkins students were seated alphabetically, and in one class Edith found herself alongside Hepburn and another student who caught her own fancy, Donald Hooker. Urged on by Kit, Edith began inviting both men to tea at the girls' apartment. From these genteel afternoon tête-á-têtes sprang two marriages that would end only in death and last a combined total of ninety years.

Born December 18, 1879, Norval Thomas Hepburn (he reversed his first and middle names at Johns Hopkins) was nearly two years younger than Kit, though by his stolid appearance, booming voice and Virginia-gentleman bearing he gave the impression of being considerably more mature. ("It was the whole package Mother fell in love with. From the beginning there was no question in her mind that he was the one and that he'd come first.")

To be sure, the Hepburns were no match for the Houghtons financially. Not even close. Nor were they among the blueblood First Families of Virginia. They could, however, trace their genealogy back to sixteenth-century Scotland and James Hepburn, fourth Earl of

Bothwell and third husband of Mary, Queen of Scots. (Katharine Hepburn would play the queen opposite Fredric March as her ancestor Bothwell in John Ford's 1936 screen version of *Mary of Scotland.*)

Tom Hepburn grew up in Still Pond, Hanover County, Virginia—seventeen miles outside Richmond and easily within earshot, his minister father often recalled, of the cannons' roar from the battlefield at Cold Harbor. It was here, on June 3, 1864, that Ulysses S. Grant attacked the heavily fortified enemy positions of Robert E. Lee. In less than thirty minutes, more than seven thousand Union and Confederate soldiers had perished.

Tom's father, the Reverend Sewell S. Hepburn, had grown up dirt-poor in Missouri and migrated east to Virginia's Hanover County just before the Civil War. He married chestnut-haired Selina Lloyd Powell, one of the prominent Richmond Powells, and took the respectable if low-paying position of rector at St. Paul's Episcopal parish. Selina's social credentials were impeccable, but they were of little real value in postwar rural Virginia, where the most that local folk could hope for was a good crop of sweet potatoes to get them through the winter. To supplement her husband's modest stipend Selina turned their clapboard rectory into a rooming house, cooking and cleaning for boarders.

There were other economies: the washcloth and the bar of soap Reverend Hepburn used for bathing were the same washcloth and bar of soap that he used to clean his teeth—an idiosyncrasy against which his granddaughter would ultimately rebel out of her own lifelong fetish for cleanliness.

Katharine Hepburn would always admire Grandpa

Hepburn's spartan philosophy. "My grandfather was a country preacher. A simple man with a very simple philosophy of life." Tall and lean with gold-rimmed spectacles and a bushy mustache, "Parson Hep" cut a quixotic figure as he ranged throughout Hanover county on horseback, spreading the gospel to black as well as white congregations in the segregated county.

Tom Hepburn was still a schoolboy when the county's only physician, Dr. Macon, died and left Parson Hep to take over. Now the proud owner of a buggy, the Reverend traveled hundreds of miles each month providing medical and dental aid to his parishioners. On a typical weekend, he would hitch up the buggy at dawn on Saturday, set out from Old Church, and pay housecalls on several farms before finally having an early supper with a member of a congregation ("or sometimes with a Good Samaritan who would care for him and his horse," a friend recalled). Then he would get back in his buggy and drive until dark, when he would stop and spend the night with another church member. The next day he would conduct morning services at, say, Fork Church. Then there would be teeth to be pulled and dressings to be checked, before he finally headed home. Parson Hep usually straggled into the house to an understanding Selina sometime Tuesday afternoon.

At 14, Tom saw the religious conviction of his father and the entire congregation put to the test. On the evening of December 23, 1893, while Parson Hep, Selena, Tom and several church members were decorating St. Paul's for the holiday, a candle overturned, igniting a Christmas wreath. Within minutes, the church was an inferno. The Hepburns and the parishioners fled to the safety of the street, where they looked on in shocked silence as the structure burned to the ground. Shaken by the disaster, Parson Hep nevertheless went ahead with Christmas services in Hanover's old brick court-house building. It would be two full years before the impoverished community could raise enough money to build a new St. Paul's on the ashes of the old. For the Reverend Hepburn's teenage son, it was a lesson in faith and grit.

Predictably, Parson Hep had hoped that his son Tom might follow in his footsteps as a preacher. He brought the boy along on his rounds, and Tom did become in-trigued—by his father's medical responsibilities, not his clerical ones. Besides, Tom had another problem with a career in the ministry: he was outspoken in his criticism of organized religion, among other established institu-tions. At every available opportunity he would rail against big business, the Republicans, and anyone who stepped on "the rights of the common man." In this conservative southern community, it was all Tom's be-leaguered parents could do just to have him keep his radical views to himself.

He didn't, but that didn't prevent his being accepted at the first Methodist university in the country, Ran-dolph-Macon College in nearby Ashland. Tom excelled both in his studies and as an all-around athlete; his pas-sion for physical fitness and discipline included starting each day with an icy shower (an addiction his daughter Kate would eventually inherit).

Hepburn also found a soapbox of sorts as editor of the *Randolph-Macon Monthly*. Under the byline "N. T. Hepburn," he wrote several editorials. In most of them he exhorted his classmates to contribute to the college's student publications or urged them to patronize local merchants who advertised in the *Monthly* and the Randolph-Macon *Annual*. Even here, however, he showed a flair for the dramatic that would be passed on to his next generation:

> Do businessmen rush up to our manager, and, with bended knee and supplicating mien, crave to be permitted to advertise? Ask your managers. After work (and hard work it is, too) they have solicited, not permitted, the advertisements. They have spent much time and endless worry that your publications may be neat and attractive in appearance and size. They have persuaded these businessmen that it will pay them to advertise. If it does not pay them, will they advertise in the future? If they do not advertise in the future, what will become of our publications? Hence we say, patronize your advertisers . . . It is your duty!

On the subject of Yuletide merrymaking:

> Within a few days, most of us will scatter to our respective homes to enjoy that most merry of seasons, Christmas . . . But let us not go to extremes. Still remember that we are college men, in whom self-control should be thoroughly established. On such occasions of world-wide merriment, the tendency is to participate in and do those things for which after

moments we feel regret and shame. As college men, we stand not only for ourselves, but for a principle. At no time should we bring that principle to shame. So let us be thoughtful in our jollity. A pleasant Christmas to you all.

Curiously, long before he met any of the Houghton women, Hepburn showed a keen awareness of the ways in which institutions of higher learning had stacked the deck against females—an awareness, he once said rather mysteriously, that grew out of his own "personal contact" with intellectually gifted women seeking full educational equality. The typically florid editorial he wrote defending a woman's right to earn a graduate school degree had a definite undercurrent of chauvinism, and by today's standards would seem hamfisted if well-meaning. But for the times, his ideas were considered nothing short of radical. More important, they were obviously heartfelt:

> To the man who expects to continue his course at post-graduate institutions, such as Columbia, Chicago, Johns Hopkins, and Stanford, the fact that there he will possibly be the fellow student of some woman is not looked forward to with a very great degree of relish. There is little doubt but that the majority of the world, both men and women, look upon the university and professional woman with harsh criticism and severe disfavor. It is with grave misgivings that we see those whom, from time immemorial, we have thought of as sisters and

daughters, wives and mothers, gradually laying claim to be no longer in need of our care and protection, but to be our competitors in the maelstrom of life. It being evident that she cannot compete with us in the field of manual work, she has naturally turned to the field of mental work.

The usual destiny of woman is to be a woman—the highest and purest destiny that God has given us. As a daughter—the fountain of beauty, merriment, and attraction in our homes. As a wife—the inspirer, sympathizer, and true companion of her husband. As a mother—the perpetuator of God's most perfect creation, the sower, teacher, and preacher of all pure and noble deeds, the true director of the tone of the intellectual world, the source of all good, next to our Creator.

The professional and higher educated woman we are ever ready to censure, but before we criticise them we ought to ask ourselves honestly why we do so blame them. Where does the trouble lie? That there is a need for the woman doctor is evidenced by the demand for them and their success. That many women have the brain and intellect to go through the mental training of the average man it is absurd to deny and narrow to argue. That some women have a sincere love of literature and science, and long to better the world by some little addition to truth, it has been our privilege to learn by personal acquaintance with such women. That they have not the structure and usually the strength to endure as prolonged a continued strain of mental work as man seems to be the hardest fact for them to realize or acknowledge.

Why cannot a man and a woman work at desks side by side, oblivious of differences in sex, as intellect with intellect, both in the pursuit of scientific truth? Here again the fault lies with the man and not the woman. He, not the woman, is not educated up to it. He, who claims to be more intellectual, cannot make the intellect rule the body, and hence imagines the occurrence of thoughts that probably have never arisen in the mind of his more innocent and intense co-worker.

Therefore, we say, because of our unjust criticism and lack of development, we should not condemn women to narrower limits than we have. Since we find co-education unsuccessful and uncongenial, we should not blame women, but give them separate buildings, lecture halls, and laboratories, all with the same advantages that we have. Instead of causing them to perform their work in the same short time that our physical strength permits us to do, extend the time to suit their strength. Let them work in an atmosphere of congeniality, not criticism. Let them feel that we not only do not criticise them, but that they have from their brother intellects best wishes for God's speed. Then, and then only, may we hope to see the possibility of the higher educated woman. Then, and then only, can many women fulfill their true destiny.

After he earned his bachelor's degree from Randolph-Macon in 1900 and his master's in pre-med from the same college the following year, Tom was bound for Johns Hopkins—and a rendezvous with a beautiful hell-raiser quite capable of fulfilling her own destiny.

Tom was secretly smitten with Kit from the start, but in his dealings with her he was exasperatingly polite. After countless teas with Edith and her beau Donald Hooker, Kit wondered if the too-gentlemanly Virginian was ever going to make his move. "He's more of a sitter," she carped to Edith, "than a suitor."

Kit was about to force his hand when Tom sprang the good news: one of the most prestigious professors at Johns Hopkins, Dr. William Halsted, had selected Tom to spend a year as a special exchange scholar in surgery at the University of Heidelberg. He was to sail for Germany in two weeks.

At first Kit did nothing to dampen Tom's enthusiasm. She, more than anyone, knew that such opportunities were rare and should be seized without hesitation. She waved goodbye to him as the train pulled out of Baltimore Station for New York, where Tom was to board a liner bound for Bremen. They wrote to one another almost daily, but as the months wore on Kit's patience wore down. Tom's letters, scrupulously formal and businesslike, showed not the slightest hint of passion or commitment. And she was not so liberated that she could confront him with *the* question directly. "The best thing about our relationship," she finally wrote, "is that whenever one of us marries, it won't hurt our relationship at all."

She was not prepared for Tom's reply. "How can you say such a thing?" he howled. "I'll never marry anyone if I don't marry you!" And that November of 1904, over Uncle Amory's anticipated objections, he did.

Some eighty years later, Kit and Tom's eldest daughter would reflect, "How goddamn lucky I was to be dealt that pair out of the shuffle."

8.

The nurse held me up
to the window so Mother
could see if I had red hair.
Dad called me "Redtop."

Even before the Reverend Sewell Hepburn presided over the marriage of his son in a small ceremony, Dr. Tom had carefully weighed his professional options. He could stay and hang out his shingle in Baltimore, or he could open up a practice in one of the big cities. Kate reflects on her father's options: "Dad had been a brilliant student and now he had a wonderful future ahead of him. He could have gone anywhere, but he did not want to function in Baltimore because he hated the thought of having family—namely my mother's sisters—around. And he didn't want to function in New York or Boston because he liked to live in the country, and both he and Mother wanted a big family. Then he met O. C. Smith . . ."

Dr. Oliver Cotton Smith, Hartford Hospital's innovative senior surgeon, was already something of a legend in the medical community when he approached Tom Hepburn about joining the Hartford staff. Smith was also a recognized expert in urology—the field that Hepburn found most intriguing. If Hepburn agreed to intern at Hartford Hospital, Smith promised him the experience—and the freedom—he would need to become one of the best urologists in the country. Edith, who had given up her own studies at Johns Hopkins to marry Donald Hooker, was among those who urged Tom to accept Smith's offer. Kit's little sister had learned much about Hartford from her own husband-to-be, whose Puritan ancestors had founded the city nearly three centuries earlier, and both Hooker and Edith felt the Hepburns would flourish there.

Predictably, there were complications. Hepburn, if he decided to take the position, would be Hartford Hospital's first married intern, and all interns were—without

exception—required to live on the premises. O. C. Smith
helped the newlyweds bend the rules. Without inform-
ing administrators, he arranged for Tom and Kit to move
into a house—actually half of a run-down red brick tenement—situated directly across from the doctors' entrance
of the hospital. The rent—thirty dollars a month—was
a bargain, even for 1904.

To answer his call-bell like any other intern, "Hep,"
as he came to be known among his colleagues, rigged
a bell and line from the interns' quarters to his bedroom.
When it rang, he dashed downstairs and sprinted across
the street. ("Daddy was so fast on his feet, nobody ever
found out where he lived.") Years later, the rule re-
quiring interns to live at the hospital was changed.

Their close proximity to the hospital did have one big
advantage for Kit; it proved especially convenient on the
morning of November 8, 1905, when she gave birth to
Thomas Houghton Hepburn.

While Kit settled into the business of motherhood,
Tom wrapped up his internship and opened up his own
office a few blocks away on High Street. It was not just
any doctor's office. At the time, specializing in surgery
was unheard of—surgeons were general practitioners
who, in addition to treating daily aches and pains, performed the occasional operation. Dr. Hepburn recognized that an explosion of knowledge was occurring in
surgical techniques and that specialization would soon
become a necessity. The more expertise a physician
achieved in surgery, the more patients would seek him
out. So Hepburn stopped treating coughs and rashes
and gout and concentrated on general surgery. It was
an extraordinary decision that would earn him the re-

spect of some of his medical colleagues and the enmity of others. (Over the years, this hostility on the part of certain members of the medical establishment would cost Dr. Hepburn several important staff appointments.)

Precisely two years after Tom's birth, on November 8, 1907, Kit Hepburn gave birth to the couple's second child and first daughter. Since their first son was named after his father, it seemed only right that the first Hepburn girl be named after her mother: Katharine. Katharine Houghton Hepburn. Little Tom had his mother's coloring, so Kit had prayed for a little girl with her husband's ruddy face and red hair. The baby let out a healthy howl. "Hold her up to the window," Kit instructed the nurse. "Hold her up to the light so I can see . . . Yes, it's red!"

To the rest of the world, she would be Kate, and to her family Kathy or Katy (pronounced Catty). But from that moment on, Dad reserved for himself the right to call her "Redtop."

9.

Some people are New York or London, or—God help them— Los Angeles. I am Hartford.

Among the many New England cities rich in history and culture, Hartford was unique. Nowhere did the roots of American democracy run deeper. Upset with the strict theological rule of the Puritan settlers in Massachusetts, renegade pastor Thomas Hooker (an ancestor of Kit's physician brother-in-law) broke away in 1636 and led his flock of independent-spirited Protestants to a Dutch trading post on the western bank of the Connecticut River. Charles II essentially gave Hartford its independence in 1662, but Sir Edmund Andros, colonial governor of New England, attempted to seize Hartford's charter. The attempt was foiled when Joseph Wadsworth hid the document in a hollow tree, known ever since as the Charter Oak.

Hartford was an important arms depot during the Revolutionary War, and in 1814 the city hosted the historic Hartford Convention. In the late eighteenth century, a group of Yale intellectuals known as the Hartford Wits conspired through satire and verse to establish the independence of American letters. Hartford native Noah Webster was one of their greatest champions. The most prolific female author of the nineteenth century, Lydia Sigourney, presided over literary salons in the mansion built for her by her millionaire husband; she came to be known throughout the United States as "the Sweet Singer of Hartford." John Pierpont Morgan, Sr. was born in Hartford, as were firearms magnate Samuel Colt (Hartford's flourishing munitions industry also produced the Sharpe rifle and the Gatling gun), the theologian Horace Bushnell, and the American historian and philosopher John Fiske. The inventor of the elevator, Elisha Graves Otis, set up shop in the city, as did the

---

liquor-importing Heublein family. Hartford's factories churned out silks and leather goods, and its buzzing subscription houses and modern printing plants made it a thriving publishing center. Hartford boasted then, as it does now, America's oldest continuously published newspaper, the *Courant*.

For all this, Hartford would owe its global fame to a single sedate business. Long before 1919, the year the 34-story, 527-foot-tall Travelers Tower began its half-century reign as New England's tallest structure (an honor today held by Boston's 60-story John Hancock Building), and even before Hartford virtually rebuilt Chicago after the Great Fire of 1871, firms with names like the Hartford, the Travelers, Aetna and Allstate had made it the insurance capital of the world.

Understandably, then, Hartford society was ruled by the princes of this multi-billion-dollar insurance industry. In a strange sort of parallel to the Hepburn/Houghton/Hooker cabal of *H*s that had resulted from the alphabetical seating arrangements at Johns Hopkins, a wildly disproportionate number of Hartford's Old Guard families possessed surnames that began with the letter *B*: the Beaches, the Brainards, the Burrs, the Battersons, the Bissells and the Bulkeleys. (A distant cousin of Kit's father, Fannie Houghton, had married Morgan Gardner Bulkeley, linking the two families; they would not become friends, however, until several years later.) Not to mention the Brewsters, Bunces and Bushnells. Intermarriage made this exclusive club even more insular, as Bulkeleys married Brainards, and Battersons wed Beaches. "The sons of Beaches," quipped one local wag, "always marry Battersons."

Another thing they had in common was a fierce pride in belonging to that stolid breed known as the Connecticut Yankee. Not to be confused with what they considered to be their less refined and softer brethren in the other New England states, *Connecticut* Yankees viewed themselves as smarter, more enterprising, tougher, more principled, better-looking—in short, in every way a cut superior.

As their fortunes grew, these families retreated west to the hills overlooking the city and the river. The massive homes with mullioned windows, columned porticoes, and jutting porte cocheres that sprang up along Woodland and Forest streets made an unmistakable statement: in Hartford, insurance is king.

Nook Farm was the glittering exception. Bordered by Farmington Avenue on the north, the Park River to the west and south, and Laurel Street on the east, this 100-acre tract was the intellectual and artistic heart of the city, a bastion of authors and activists who had fallen heir to the tradition of Noah Webster and the Hartford Wits. It was here, among massive Victorians and sprawling clapboard "cottages," that Harriet Beecher Stowe lived out her last twenty-six years. It was natural for the author of *Uncle Tom's Cabin* to settle here: before the Civil War, several Nook Farm houses actually served as stations on the abolitionist Underground Railroad. And it was here too that Harriet's independent-minded sister Isabella Beecher Hooker forged the state's Woman Suffrage Movement, that United States Senator Francis Gillette mapped out the strategy of the abolitionists in Congress, and that Senator Gillette's son William grew up to be one of the most popular actors of his day, known best for his portrayal of Sherlock Holmes on Broadway and on stages throughout the world.

All were content to live in the looming shadow of Nook Farm's most celebrated resident, who had been lured to Hartford in 1871 by the promise of a juicy publishing contract and stayed for thirty-one years. Mark Twain was so impressed by Hartford's solid wealth and moral uprightness ("I desire to have the respect of this sterling old Puritan community, for their respect is well worth having") that he plunked down $31,000 for a five-acre lot at 351 Farmington Avenue and spent another $100,000 to construct a three-story, nineteen-room, five-bath mansion as whimsical as it was grand. A Hansel and Gretel hodgepodge of balconies, gables, fifty-foot-high octagonal turrets and chimneys, the house that Samuel Clemens built also featured a pavilion-sized enclosure that he called an "Ombra" (derived from *umbra*, Latin for shadow or shaded area), a roof of colored tile, Victorian gingerbread detailing, and a geometric design that zigzagged around the structure's black- and red-brick exterior. Such grandeur demanded a suitably large household staff. Twain's included a butler, laundress, cook, nanny, housemaid, and coachman.

The Prince and the Pauper, A Connecticut Yankee in King Arthur's Court, and *Tom Sawyer* were all published while Twain lived at Nook Farm. And so was *Huckleberry Finn.* (Though he had heard about them since his Missouri boyhood, Twain had never actually *seen* huckleberries until he moved to Hartford, where they abounded.)

What Twain found at Nook Farm was a cozy enclave of kindred spirits in the midst of Hartford's bristling commerce. It was a place where neighbors whose brains were at least as impressive as their bank balances wandered in and out of one another's palatial homes without ringing, and communed over billiards, teas, and games of whist. There were musicales and the sort of discussion groups where Kit Houghton—had she lived in Hartford at the time, and had women been allowed to participate—would have felt right at home. The most exclusive of these was the all-male, twenty-member Monday Evening Club, into which Twain was immediately inducted.

Of all his Nook Farm cronies, Twain grew especially close to Charles Dudley Warner. A onetime lawyer turned *Courant* editor, Warner had arrived at Nook Farm five years earlier, purchased the rambling "cottage" at 133 Hawthorn Street from Harriet Beecher Stowe's brother-in-law Thomas Clapp Perkins, and set out to fashion a literary reputation for himself. Here he wrote *My Summer in a Garden*, a collection of travel essays that attracted considerable attention when it was published in 1871. Twain's arrival that year also meant that at last Warner had someone to share his dissatisfaction with the state of contemporary fiction. It was during one of their long, languid dinners to while away the cold winter months that Warner and Twain, at the urging of their exasperated wives, agreed to do something about it.

It is astonishing when considered today that Twain's fame up until this time rested entirely on his nonfiction work; neither he nor Warner had even attempted a novel before, but together they would write a fictional account of nineteenth-century greed and its heavy spiritual toll. They called it *The Gilded Age*.

Warner died in October of 1900, and soon thereafter Twain sold his house to the president of the Hartford

Fire Insurance Company, John Bissell. Yet when the Hepburns in turn bought and moved into "the Warner House" at 133 Hawthorn Street, they might still have heard the faint echoes of Twain and Warner meeting each night in the parlor to read their day's work to one another and to their wives.

The house itself, which stood precisely the same as it had that bright afternoon in 1863 when Harriet Beacher Stowe sketched it for posterity, more than lived up to the orphan's dream of hearth and home that Kit held close. Designed by the English architect Octavius Augustus Jordon, who specialized in creating English-style country cottages in the wealthier American suburbs, 133 Hawthorn sat back on two acres dotted with evergreens, birches, and maples. A gravel drive wound up to the three-story red brick Victorian Gothic structure, with its main gable directly above the covered front entrance flanked by two smaller peaked gables, all bordered with lacy Victorian black trim. Two brick chimneys poked through the pitched roof, and all the windows were dressed up with shiny black shutters. A lush network of vines covered the west wall entirely and crept around to the front, encroaching on the view from the topmost window.

Inside, the main rooms were large and inviting. Off the parlor was a plant-filled conservatory with a glass dome and floor-to-ceiling windows that swung out onto the backyard with its wooden garden swing, shingle-roofed doghouse, and pitted terrain. The yard was bordered on the south by railroad tracks. On the other side of the tracks were the buckled ruins of an ancient tennis court. Beyond sprawled Brownie Park, where the Hepburn kids would "sail" their own small raft on the park's pond (which, despite the general affluence of the area, was home to a sizable population of rats). A brook snaked languidly along the lot's eastern perimeter, its banks sprinkled with daffodils and tiger lilies.

Taken as a whole, the property had a certain off-center charm about it—like a sweetly eccentric maiden aunt barely tolerated by the stately dowagers down the street.

If a single feature of the house could sum up its significance to the Hepburn Family it was the line Charles Dudley Warner had inscribed above the marble mantlepiece in Dr. Hepburn's study: *Listen to the Song of Life.* "I saw that every day for as long as I can remember," says Kate. "First, when I was maybe four or five, I'd stare at it and stare at it and ask Mother and Dad over and over again what it meant. Then it hit me, Oh, *that's* what it means! We all believed that was the only way to live. From the moment she set foot in that house, Mother knew this was a perfect place for her to raise her family. And that's all she wanted to do with the rest of her life. At least, that's what Mother *thought.*"

10

Venereal disease was not exactly considered a polite topic. This was something you just did not talk about, period. The medical profession thought it was best ignored. Daddy felt otherwise.

For the Hepburns' first year there, life at 133 Hawthorn was every bit as perfect as Kit had imagined it would be. Though Hep's income as a surgeon amounted to a meager $2,000 for the entire year of 1908, he proved an adept neophyte in the world of finance. Through a series of shrewd investments, he parlayed his wife's modest share of the Houghton holdings into a substantial fortune—more than enough to pay for a household staff that included a maid, a cook, and a nanny. ("You didn't have to be really rich to afford help back then. The going *weekly* rate was only five dollars for a cook and three dollars for a maid. If you had any money at all, you were just sort of expected to hire servants.") Actually, the Hepburn household staff was quite modest for the place and the time; the staunchly upright Bissells had never carried fewer than a dozen employees on the domestic payroll.

While Kit immersed herself in the day-to-day business of running her household, her husband divided his seven-day work week between his small, renegade surgical practice on High Street and assisting his mentor O.C. Smith in the operating room at Hartford Hospital. Urology as a science was in its infancy; for years the medical establishment steadfastly refused to recognize it as an independent surgical specialty (Hartford Hospital would eventually become one of the first facilities in the country to do so by establishing a full-fledged urology department in 1935). But the powers-that-be at Hartford Hospital did grudgingly permit the zealous young doctor to launch a urology department as an adjunct to general surgery. Along with Dr. Arthur C. Heublein, whose family name was to become more famous for the exporting of liquor than for championing the cause of medical science, Hep also pioneered the use of X-rays as a diagnostic tool—a notion that at first was cooly received by his foot-dragging superiors. "All apparatus was paid for by me," Dr. Hepburn later recalled with more than a hint of asperity, "as the hospital authorities considered the procedures relatively useless."

The focus of Dr. Hepburn's indignation shifted dramatically one afternoon in the spring of 1910, when a well-spoken young woman with porcelain-perfect features and a dazzling social pedigree arrived at his office on the arm of her husband, a fast-rising insurance executive. They were in their early twenties, attractive, charming, affluent—precisely the kind of referral patients Tom Hepburn had hoped to attract. While the woman's husband smoked a cigarette in the waiting room, Hep listened in disbelief as she matter-of-factly informed him she was suffering from syphilis. Her husband of six months had been infected the night before their wedding, she calmly explained, when he and his ushers had indulged in a wild stag party at a downtown whorehouse. She had forgiven him completely, and they still loved one another. Now it was up to the good doctor to cure them both. They were eager to start a family.

Hep tried with the husband and succeeded, but hers was a particularly virulent case. One evening she arrived complaining of stabbing abdominal pains. Before she could finish, Hep's beautiful patient collapsed. She died not long after.

Kit, who had gotten to know the young woman, was shattered by the news. For Hep, the woman's tragic death marked nothing less than a turning point.

Nationwide estimates of death from venereal disease ran into the tens of thousands, with an equal number of "survivors" of syphilitic infection living out the remainder of their lives in Hogarthian insane asylums. Each year thousands of children born to infected mothers arrived blind or with some other severe birth defect. The numbers were staggering, especially in light of the fact that venereal disease was largely preventable through the use of condoms (though the use of sulfa drugs to combat certain forms of VD was still years away).

Yet for all its staggering toll in human misery, venereal disease remained a subject so taboo that even physicians were loathe to discuss it among themselves, much less take a public stand. In a society where exposing the female ankle was considered risqué, no one—not even doctors—easily acknowledged the existence of genitalia. More to the point, people of quality did not get the disease—an assumption that even Dr. Hepburn made before he encountered the lovely young society matron with the fatal case of syphilis.

"Dad set out to find out more about venereal disease," says Kate, "and was absolutely stunned to learn that Hartford was the center of the white-slave trade on the East Coast. There were endless houses of prostitution in tenements that turned out to be owned by some of Hartford's 'best' families. The police just looked the other way rather than ruffle the wrong feathers."

Across the United States, the prevalence of prostitution was enormous. An estimated sixty thousand girls under the age of twenty joined the swelling ranks of the world's oldest profession every year—each with the capacity to transmit life-threatening disease to hundreds

Amory Houghton Sr., Kate's great-grandfather and the founder of Corning Glass, and his son Amory Jr., uncle of Kate's mother, "Kit" Houghton, and a great influence on Kit's life. *The Archives of the Corning Glass Works.*

Mark Twain and family at Nook Farm in Hartford, Connecticut. *Mark Twain Memorial, Hartford, Ct.*

Front and rear views of the Hepburn house at 133 Hawthorn. *The Stowe-Day Foundation.*

The Reverend Sewell Hepburn, Kate's paternal grandfather. *Steven Colvin.*

Dr. Thomas Hepburn, Kate's father, in a picture taken for his graduation from the medical college of Johns Hopkins University, 1905. *The Alan Mason Chesney Medical Archives of the Johns Hopkins Medical Institutions.*

George Bernard Shaw, circa 1910. *The Bettmann Archive.*

Kate at 2½, with older brother Tom. *The Homer Dickens Collection.*

Kit Hepburn (front row in light dress) with fellow suffrage leaders, 1912. *Archives, History and Genealogy Unit, Connecticut State Library.*

Kate at 4, alone and with 6-year-old Tom. *The Homer Dickens Collection.*

Emma Goldman at a suffrage street rally, circa 1912. *The Bettman Archive.*

Kit marching in the front row (far right) of a Hartford suffrage parade, 1912. *Archives, History and Genealogy Unit, Connecticut State Library.*

Hartford, 1912: Children play outside brothel (on right of shop) soon to be closed as a result of Kit's anti-prostitution campaign. *Archives, History and Genealogy Unit, Connecticut State Library.*

Emmeline Pankhurst. *The Bettmann Archive.*

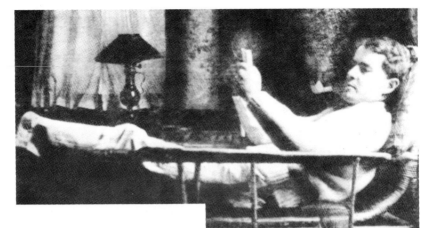

Dr. Tom Hepburn, circa 1913. *The Homer Dickens Collection.*

Kit Hepburn with her children, 1916. Kate, at 8, is on right, Tom on left, Dick and Bob in foreground. *The Homer Dickens Collection.*

of customers in the course of her "career." But Dr. Hepburn was less worried about these women and their clients than he was about the unsuspecting wives who waited at home, oblivious to the microscopic threat that carried with it the grim promise of debilitation and death. Clearly something had to be done to warn people—good, morally upright people—of the very real danger.

Hep and a small group of associates from the hospital banded together to found an organization to combat the problem. But what to call it? Any blatant reference to venereal disease was out. So was the word *sex* or any variation thereof. *Social hygiene* seemed inoffensive enough. They called their organization the Connecticut Social Hygiene Association.

The problem remained: How was Hep to get the message across to a public that devoutly believed "It can never happen to me"? The answer came in the unlikely form of a bewhiskered Irish playwright named George Bernard Shaw. ("Daddy was completely *crazy* about him way before anybody else in Hartford had even heard of Shaw.") The young doctor had devoured all of his work, and when he learned that Shaw had written the preface for a daring play dealing with venereal disease by the French dramatist Eugène Brieux, Hep, says his daughter, "rushed right out and bought a copy." The play, translated by Shaw's wealthy, high-born Irish wife, Charlotte Payne-Townshend, was called *Damaged Goods*, and its subject—syphilis—had triggered a *petit scandale* on the other side of the Atlantic. Hep read *Damaged Goods* in a single sitting, then dashed off a letter to Shaw himself. ("Dad thought *Damaged Goods* would be a fantastic way to get his message across in an effective way without turning people off. To really grab them. So he wrote Shaw asking for permission to reprint it here, and Shaw saw to it that he got it. Then Dad borrowed some money to have a few hundred copies made and distributed throughout this country.") Thus began a fond correspondence between Shaw and Hep that was to last for decades. "Dad was such a nut, he destroyed all the correspondence," Kate says with a sigh. "Destroyed it all—just tore it up and threw it away. Can you believe it? The important thing to Dad was that he be unencumbered by old letters, so he never saved anything. 'Don't clutter up your life,' he'd always say. But it's sad, isn't it?"

Damaged Goods nudged the door open a crack, but Hepburn knew that it would take a well-organized national effort to force Americans to face up to the venereal-disease epidemic in their midst. Such an organization would need a strong, nationally revered figure at its helm, and Hep knew just the man for the post. He boarded the 10 A.M. train for Boston and that afternoon was sitting in the Cambridge office of Charles Eliot, President Emeritus of Harvard University.

Eliot, himself a scientist by training, was widely regarded as the foremost educator of the age—and with good reason. From 1869 to 1909, he had guided Harvard's evolution from a relatively modest college with affiliated professional schools into a great modern institution that could hold its own against the finest European universities. Eliot had also been an ardent supporter of Elizabeth Cary Agassiz in her crusade to establish Radcliffe as a woman's college with strong ties to Harvard.

When Dr. Thomas Hepburn introduced himself to Eliot that afternoon, the eminent academician was in the process of closing the Harvard chapter of his distinguished career. Unbeknownst to his young visitor from Hartford, Eliot was about to clean out his desk in preparation for a new and no less challenging job. Yet he listened, patient if expressionless, while Hep delivered his impassioned plea. When Hep at last finished, Dr. Eliot stood and picked up a piece of paper that had been lying on his desk. "This is my letter to the president accepting my appointment as United States Ambassador to the Court of St. James's."

Hep's heart sank.

"I'm not going to mail it. I'll be more useful doing the work you've just described."

Thus was born the American Social Hygiene Association, with the illustrious Charles Eliot as its president.

Eliot's powers of persuasion proved to be less formidable than Hepburn's: he could not talk Hep into taking the job of executive secretary, even at five times his surgeon's income. "Daddy always believed that if you stick to one thing—*one thing*—long enough, and work at it hard enough, you might even get it right," says Kate. "For him that one thing was being a surgeon— the very best damn surgeon he could possibly be. Do you suppose I take after him in that respect?"

11.

I don't think he leaned toward
Communism. Mother did . . .

By the autumn of 1909, Kit Houghton Hepburn was growing increasingly restless. To be sure, there had been occasional flashes of the old, rabble-rousing Kit since the move to 133 Hawthorn. Certainly she had fully supported her husband's crusade against venereal disease. And one morning, after Kit had become aware that workers at the two nonunion plants down Hawthorn Street—Arrow Electric and Hart & Hegeman—were forced to squat on sidewalks and perch on fences to eat their lunches out of paper bags and battered pails, she trotted over to the foreman and invited his men to dine *al fresco* on the grounds at 133 Hawthorn.

When Dr. Hepburn returned from work that afternoon, he beheld a wasteland of trampled hedges, fallen tree limbs, and overturned lawn furniture. Broken bottles, newspapers, and half-eaten sandwiches were strewn about. One of the windows on the south side of the house was broken, casualty of an impromptu lunchtime game of catch.

Inside the house, Kit was fuming. She told Hep of her generous offer to the plant workers and how they in her absence away for lunch had chosen to show their gratitude by reenacting the sacking of Troy. Instead of exploding, Dr. Hepburn calmly lit his pipe. "Well, my dear," he said between puffs, "now you've learned something about the differences between having principles and acting on them."

Still, something gnawed at her insides. Her daughter Kate recalls Kit's moment of truth: "So there was Mother walking around the streets of Hartford holding onto my brother Tom with one hand and pushing me in my pram with the other and suddenly it hit her: 'Yes, this is all very nice. But is this *it*? Is this what I am going to do with the rest of my life?' "

Kit's sister Edith had already shown the way. After dropping out of medical school to marry Donald Hooker, Edith had founded the Guild of St. George, a home for unwed mothers in Baltimore. Watching scores of young girls file in and out of the home, Edith finally became convinced that a society controled by men was insensitive to their plight. "The enfranchisement of women," Edith wrote her older sister, "is the first step in improving moral conditions." She urged Kit to join the suffrage fight with her.

Kit was not at all certain that she could make a significant contriution or that she should even try—until a grandmotherly Englishwoman named Emmeline Pankhurst set foot on American soil for the first time in the fall of 1908. Pankhurst was anything but imposing: when she debarked in New York, newspaper reporters described her as wearing a felt hat, a purple chiffon scarf, and an ivy-leaf geranium in the lapel of her blue serge suit. Yet in the six years since she and a half-dozen friends had gathered in the parlor of her Manchester home to form the Women's Social and Political Union, Emmeline Pankhurst had led a passionate, sometimes bloody war for equality that had rocked Britain to its foundations.

At first glance, the tiny (5 feet 2 inches), refined-looking English lady seemed an unlikely firebrand. A daughter of social reformers, Emmeline Goulden married activist lawyer Richard Marsden Pankhurst in 1879. Destitute after his sudden death in 1898, and with a young family to support, Mrs. Pankhurst took a position as registrar of births and deaths at Rusholme. In 1903 she, along with her daughters Christabel (who was eventually made a Dame of the British Empire) and Sylvia, founded the Women's Social and Political Union.

Five years later, the Pankhursts' illegal picketing led to Emmeline's first arrest and three month's imprisonment in Holloway Gaol. That, in turn, triggered more violent tactics: railway stations, race-course stands, even a house being constructed for Prime Minister Lloyd George at Walton Heath, were set ablaze. Storefront windows in London were smashed, and a bomb was planted in St. Paul's Cathedral. These acts, for which Mrs. Pankhurst accepted full responsibility, made her the epicenter of the suffrage storm.

Ever since the Arrow-Hart debacle, Hep had been aware that his wife was not entirely satisfied with her quiet life at Nook Farm. When he read in the *Hartford Courant* that Emmeline Pankhurst, after making several appearances in New York, would be speaking in Hartford, he urged his wife to go.

Pankhurst's reputation had preceded her to America, but she could not have anticipated the scene that awaited her at Carnegie Hall. "The huge hall was entirely filled," the militant suffragette later wrote, "and an enormous crowd of people thronged the streets outside for blocks." There were familiar faces on the podium, but, Pankhurst remembered, "the great crowd before me was made up of strangers, and I could not know how they would respond to my story." As she rose to speak, a deep hush fell over the crowd. "I am," said Pankhurst, "what you call a hooligan." Carnegie Hall exploded with laughter and applause.

No such triumph awaited Pankhurst in conservative Hartford, where Kit was among a smattering of women who showed up at the 1,620-seat Parsons Theatre to hear Pankhurst speak. But she was no less a spellbinder that evening. "There were only about two hundred people in the audience," Kit would recall, "and she gave one of the most remarkable speeches I have ever heard. I came away determined to work for votes for women. I had been intellectually convinced for some time, but it took that speech to stir me to action. Another girl in the audience had the same reaction. She wrote on a piece of paper, 'I wish to devote my life to this cause,' and gave it to Mrs. Pankhurst." The young woman was a grade-school teacher named Emily Pierson, and for the next twelve years she and Kit would work shoulder to shoulder for the right to vote.

That afternoon at 5:00, over tea and cinnamon toast, Hep listened to Kit recite passages from Pankhurst's speech. He could not remember the last time his wife was so fired up. She *had* to join the movement. But there was a hitch. While Hartford did harbor a few enlightened souls—it was here at Nook Farm, after all, that Isabella Beecher Hooker had founded the state's women's suffrage movement three years after the close of the Civil War—suffragettes were largely frowned upon, even feared, in this rigidly Republican community. "Mother told Daddy that she wanted to get into the movement," says Kate Hepburn, "and that she couldn't care less if it meant being snubbed by some of the snootier neighbors. But she did worry that it 'might' wreck her husband's career."

"No 'might' about it," Hep shot back. "Of course it

will hurt, but do it anyway. If I can't succeed anyway, then I deserve to fail. Life isn't worth living unless you do what you believe in. Jump into the fray!"

"How Daddy dared to do what he did I just don't know," Kate reflects. "He didn't have that much money at the beginning, and he was really taking a gamble that Mother's involvement wouldn't cost him patients. But he never regretted Mother's decision to take up the fight. Never. He reveled in it."

12.

There was a group that thought
Mother and Dad were great,
and there was a group that
thought they were hotheads.
Both groups were right.

For all their dedication to the suffrage cause, Kit and her new comrade-in-arms Emily Pierson had to admit they "knew nothing about the subject except that we believed in it with a passion." First step: "We decided to learn to speak. No one wanted to hear us, of course. We subscribed for a paper called the *Woman's Journal*, published in Boston by Alice Stowe Blackwell. I don't remember how we heard of it. We got a lot of arguments for votes for women out of it. I was to speak on woman suffrage and the home, Emily on working women and the vote. If we could only find an audience!"

In desperation, Kit turned to her cook, a black woman named Ida, and asked if she and Miss Pierson might speak at her church on the topic of votes for women. Ida arranged for the minister to drop by 133 Hawthorn, and over a pot of tea Kit persuaded him to make the church available at 3 P.M. the following Sunday. That fateful afternoon, Kit was "in utter terror when I saw the little sign outside the church saying, 'At 3 o'clock Mrs. Hepburn and Miss Pierson will speak here on Woman Suffrage.' I felt as if I should faint. My knees ached as I went up the walk to the door. I had hardly slept a wink the night before, and although I had learned my speech by heart I was not at all sure that I could remember it when face to face with an audience.

"We entered the church at three o'clock exactly, and there was no one in the church except one large black woman asleep in the back of the church. What a blessed relief! We had our meeting. I spoke for half an hour and Emily was the audience; and then Emily spoke and I was the audience. Then we waited. We thought that if we waited long enough our audience might come, and they did. By five o'clock the church was full and we had the meeting and got lots of signatures to little cards saying, *I believe in votes for women.* Our meeting was an outstanding success."

That evening, Kit and Emily Pierson formed the Equal Franchise League, which would eventually come to be known by another name: the League of Women Voters.

Kit's ferociously intense involvement in the suffrage movement did not preclude her interest in the two social issues Hep had confronted—venereal disease and prostitution. Indeed, she saw her issues and his being inexorably intertwined. Not long after Kit delivered her maiden speech, the Hepburns were invited to dinner by their neighbors the Bissells, then regarded as the leaders of Hartford society. Unlike the financially plagued Mr. Clemens, the Bissells could easily afford to furnish and maintain the Mark Twain house in grand style. A household battalion served the guests a princely meal, and then, as was the custom, the men retired upstairs to the billiard room for cigars and brandy while the ladies withdrew to the parlor.

Here were the most wealthy and powerful couples in Hartford, and Kit was not about to pass up the chance to proselytize. While the naive wives sat in stunned silence, Kit held forth on the evils of prostitution and Hartford's own notorious white-slave trade. She also spared them none of the clinical details in describing the medical effects of syphilis and gonorrhea, and alerted her listeners to the fact that wandering husbands were bringing these and other venereal diseases into the best of homes. No one was immune. Once the color had returned to the ladies' faces, someone changed the subject.

The next day, as Kate tells it, one of the wives paid a call on Kit and urged her to drop the cause. " 'All the Right People have found you and the doctor perfectly charming and enjoyed your company immensely,' the woman said. 'But they are all against this votes-for-women thing. If you persist, the invitations to dinners and dances will stop. You will become social outcasts.' " After the woman left, Kit decided that if fighting for the right to vote meant not having to go to dinner parties to be bored senseless, it wasn't much of a price to pay. Mrs. Bissell turned out to be not nearly so rigid as the visitor. When she telephoned Kit to apologize for not being able to invite her to a function because of the row it would inevitably cause among her stuffier guests, Kit had a solution: "Look", Kit told her, "why don't you ask us over alone, because we love your company and we'd love to talk. That way you don't have to worry about anyone getting all riled up." From that point on, whenever the Bissells and Hepburns saw one another they were a foursome.

Soon, Hartford society was split down the middle on the troublemaking Hepburns. ("There were actually rival factions—a great division between the people who believed in what my parents were trying to do, and the people who thought you should just shut up.") Hep also began to feel a decided chill among his colleagues at the hospital. ("Some of the other doctors wouldn't talk to Dad at all unless they were discussing a patient's condition.") No matter. Hep told his wife to keep up the good work.

For her part, Kit thought it only logical that well-heeled women should feel less than disenfranchised. In the first of many letters she would write to the *New York Times*, Kit noted:

> Women of great wealth are not dependent upon the community to any such extent as are working women and mothers of families with limited incomes, and so it is quite logical that, from a purely selfish point of view, they should not take so great an interest in woman suffrage.
>
> Women working outside the home, of whom there are over five million in the United States, feel the need of the ballot very keenly to control their conditions of work and hours. It is quite natural that they should take more of an interest in the suffrage movement than a woman who expects to spend the winter at Palm Beach.
>
> Mothers of families with small incomes are dependent upon the community for proper building laws, sanitary laws, public playgrounds, schools, public hospitals, etc. Is it strange that they should desire the vote more seriously than women who by their wealth control the conditions under which their children grow up?
>
> Besides, an increasing number of wealthy women do want to vote, notably those who are working to improve the conditions of the poor.
>
> *Katharine Houghton Hepburn*
> Jan. 21, 1909

Not all resistance, Kit soon discovered, came from outside the movement. Harriet Beecher Stowe's sister Isabella Beecher Hooker, one of the country's acknowledged leaders of the suffrage movement, died in 1907 and was succeeded by Annie Eliot Trumbull as president of the Connecticut Suffrage Association. Married to a descendant of Connecticut's Jonathan Trumbull, George Washington's close ally and the only governor of the thirteen original colonies to side with the revolutionists in the War of Independence, Annie Trumbull was an imperious, intellectually rigid social pillar and a staunch member of the conservative Asylum Hill Congregational Church. (Mark Twain had had a name for the imposing, spired stone edifice that rose just a few blocks from Nook Farm. He called Asylum Hill the "Church of the Holy Speculators.") In short, despite her involvement in an unpopular cause, no one in proper society challenged the respectability of the stolid Mrs. Trumbull.

With good reason. While she and the other association leaders—women like herself, fifty years of age or older— welcomed Kit and her eager young cohorts and even invited them to sit on the board, she insisted they comport themselves in a ladylike fashion. Fiery rhetoric, rallies, and marches were unseemly, crass, and unacceptable for women of "quality."

Kit and her fellow rebels were mystified. Surely this was a hot political issue, not an academic one. Like Emmeline Pankhurst, they believed that this was a battle to be fought at the barricades. When the *New York Times* reported that Pankhurst was to make her second trip to the United States, Kit proposed that she be invited to speak again in Hartford. Mrs. Trumbull and the Old Guard refused. Pankhurst was a militant and a radical, and they wanted nothing to do with her.

Kit decided a coup was called for and set out to line up support. At the next board meeting, held in the Hepburn parlor, she sprang her trap. In a surprise vote, Trumbull and her clique were thrown off the board. Kit took over as president, with her next-door neighbor Josephine Day Bennett as vice-president (Mrs. Bennett's main claim to fame until then was that as the daughter of the man who manufactured Pope-Hartford automobiles she was the first woman in Hartford to drive).

Just as Hep returned home from the hospital that evening, he was pushed aside by a livid Mrs. Trumbull and her enraged followers stomping out of the house. "Now, ladies," Kit said to the new majority without missing a beat, "the first new order of business is to invite Emmeline Pankhurst to speak in Hartford. All in favor . . ."

Pankhurst accepted the invitation, more heartfelt than the first she had received to come to Hartford, and Kit began planning a huge downtown parade to welcome her. But it would be an expensive undertaking, she realized, and without the financial backing of Mrs. Trumbull and her Old Guard for a time it looked as if indeed they would have to cancel. At the last minute, Kit received an envelope from Mrs. Appleton Hillyer, wealthy daughter of the prominent theologian (and ardent suffrage foe) Horace Bushnell. It contained more than enough cash to cover the association's outstanding expenses, and a letter pledging as much money as the suffragettes needed in the future—so long as her identity remain their little secret.

Pankhurst was stunned by her second reception in Hartford. She was met at the train station by Kit, who rode alongside in the parade that jammed downtown traffic for two hours. This time, the Parsons Theatre was packed with women of Hartford eager to hear the famous British suffragette. That night, Pankhurst stayed at the Hepburns' (as she would during every future trip she made to the United States). She recalled the pathetic turnout in Hartford only one year before, and marveled at the change. She knew whom to thank for it.

Atop her dresser table, Kit placed a framed quotation from Shaw: "This is the true joy of life, the being used for a purpose recognized by yourself as a mighty one; the being thoroughly worn out before you are thrown on the scrap heap; the being a force of Nature, instead of a selfish little clod of ailments and grievances complaining that the world will not devote itself to making you happy."

WOMEN IN INDUSTRY

She Is There to Stay, and She Needs the Suffrage

To the Editor of The New York Times:

In an editorial entitled "The Hardiness of Woman," you show by statistics that the entrance of women into industry has had a disastrous effect on their health and shortened their lives, and you draw the conclusion that women should not be burdened with the vote. The conclusion that I should draw from your premise would be that women apparently need the protection of the vote.

If women's health is injured by their present conditions of work, then for the good of the human race something must be done about it. Either women must be forced out of industry or special legislation must be enacted to protect women workers.

Now, one of the best ways of improving the conditions under which any class works is to give that class suffrage. Legislators make the laws regulating the conditions of work and hours in the factories, and legislators naturally pay most attention to the interests of those who elect them. If the workers are women and are therefore in need of special legislation for the protection of their health, one of the surest ways of securing that legislation is to make the legislators dependent on the votes of women as well as men for continuance of office.

Justice Brewer of the United States Supreme Court, in upholding the constitutionality of the Oregon law limiting the hours of women laundry workers to ten hours a day, said: "Her physical structure and a proper discharge of maternal functions—having in mind not merely her own health, but the well-being of the human race—justify legislation to protect her from the greed as well as the passion of man." Justice Brewer believes in woman suffrage as a potent factor in securing such legislation.

Katharine Houghton Hepburn
Hartford, Conn.

The appearance of Kit's second editorial in the *Times*
marked total Hepburn commitment to the cause. The
whole family was pressed into service. Dad sat on the
floor and stenciled VOTES FOR WOMEN on placards.
Tom, now five, and Kathy, three, tagged along, sitting
crosslegged on the platform while Mother delivered her
fiery oratory in one city after another. They even
marched behind her, wrapped in the purple, green, and
white banners of the suffrage movement, toting signs
and passing out leaflets as she picketed for votes. Tom
was on the shy side, but little Kathy was an eager lieutenant in Kit's battles.

During one of their frequent jaunts to Washington to
protest at the White House, Kit and Kathy held their
pickets high as President and Mrs. Wilson walked past.
As one of the protesters later recalled, "Mrs. Wilson
passed with a contemptuous sniff, but the president was
a gentleman. He lifted his hat and said, 'Good day,
ladies.'" Kate says that picketing alongside Mother
"seemed perfectly natural, because we were always involved in it all. It was just part of the fabric of our childhood."

Then, smack in the midst of Mother's crusades, Richard Houghton Hepburn was born. It did nothing to slow
Kit down. She waited only six weeks after the infant's

arrival to hit the streets again, bringing tiny Dick along to her meetings, leaving him with a nurse in an ante-room, and unself-consciously excusing herself whenever the need arose to nurse the baby.

No one was more enraged by all of this than *Courant* editor Charles Hopkins Clark, a revered journalist who violently opposed the suffrage movement—and who had come to detest Kit. His editorials became so bitter that they created a backlash. In one, for example, Clark argued that the only people who supported Kit and the movement were "immigrants from other states and countries." Kit in turn described Clark's jingoistic remark as "insulting," and to judge by the number of new volunteers who then came knocking on Kit's door, many *Courant* readers agreed with her.

Kit's wardrobe of pastel satin dresses and stylish, broad-brimmed hats—not to mention the same eye-catching face and figure her movie-star daughter would be blessed with—made her a standout among the frump-ish ladies who still dominated the movement. Which of course made her even more suspect to the narrow-minded likes of Clark. The *Courant*'s most vicious per-sonal attack on Kit Hepburn came in the form of an ed-itorial that asked why two young married women—namely Kit and Josephine Day Bennett—were down at the state capital during the legislative session and what they were doing for two or three hours at a time behind closed doors with senators and representatives.

Kit and her comrades had fully anticipated that their mere presence in this male bastion would be enough to raise eyebrows, and had been scrupulously careful never to enter a private office in the capital; they did all their lobbying in the hallways and lobbies, usually in full view of scores of passersby. When the *Courant* editorial appeared, the generous Mrs. Appleton Hillyer urged Kit to sue for libel, but Kit viewed Clark's vindictiveness as a welcome sign that at last she was being taken seriously—that the authorities were feeling threatened by the suffragists' growing power. "Silly, isn't it?" the unflappable Mrs. Hepburn replied to Mrs. Hillyer. "They must have needed something to print." Impressed anew, Mrs. Appleton Hillyer sat down on the spot and wrote out another fat check—her biggest contribution yet.

Not that Kit didn't strike back—in her own manner. In the summer of 1910 she hit the Connecticut circuit with a vengeance, touring church fairs and town fairs in Josephine Day Bennett's huge black Pope-Hartford limousine, a car with a tonneau that could fold back into the ideal speaker's platform. Crocker, the Bennett's chauffeur, was nowhere to be found during the speeches. He was so mortified that he made a point of losing himself in the crowd until the whole embarrassing spectacle was over. At each of their appearances, the main prop was a makeshift polling booth topped with a sign that read:

WOMEN, CHILDREN, IDIOTS AND CRIMINALS
VOTE HERE!
OUR CANDIDATE IS THE EDITOR OF THE
HARTFORD *COURANT*,
CHARLES HOPKINS CLARK

Later that summer, Kit led a "Suffrage Spectacular" parade down New York City's Fifth Avenue. It was practically unheard of for men to participate in suffrage demonstrations, but one male who did join in was the renowned educator John Dewey. Professor Dewey, a dapper little man with a fondness for brown suits and derbies, shook Kit's hand, darted over to a pile of placards, grabbed one and proceeded to march. He hadn't expected a particularly warm reception from the crowd that lined the parade route, but why, he wondered, was he being singled out for hoots and catcalls? Dewey stopped wondering when he looked up at his placard. "MEN VOTE," the sign proclaimed, "WHY CAN'T WE?"

13.

Mother always had fascinating
people over, and we kids
—how should I put this—
were told to shut up.

It was a time of bandstands, white linen suits, and straw boaters. Of Gibson girls, Model A's, and nickel cigars. Of Strauss's *Der Rosenkavalier*, Irving Berlin's "Alexander's Ragtime Band," and Stravinsky's *The Rite of Spring*. Of Amundsen's arrival at the South Pole. And of the Triangle Shirtwaist Fire.

No one found the era more exhilarating, or more perfectly suited to her iconoclastic temperament, than Kit. Her involvement in the suffrage movement had brought her in contact with a whole new world of ideas and people—of rebels like herself. To the abject horror of the righteous Mrs. Bissell and her group, Kit threw open the doors of 133 Hawthorn to freethinkers, socialists, and misfits of every stripe. Clad in a flowing silk Chinese tea robe embroidered with birds and flowers ("Mother's Mandarin outfit"), Kit presided over what would be described as Hartford's answer to Mme de Stael's salon. The Hepburn children, meantime, sat quietly in the wings. ("I was very young then—four, I guess—but I remember *lavender* clothes. We were not precocious around Mother's guests. We weren't *featured*, by any means. It wasn't that they felt particularly that children should be seen and not heard, but that the interesting person should talk, and not some dunce, which we all were. We were not starred, in other words. But we were allowed to keep our mouths shut and listen.")

Emmeline Pankhurst and her daughter Sylvia were to be frequent guests between their stays in prison. So was the controversial social reformer Charlotte Perkins Gilman.

A Hartford native, the grandniece of Harriet Beecher Stowe and a distant cousin of Kit's, Gilman knew her way around Nook Farm in general and the Hepburn house in particular; this had, after all, been the home of her older brother Thomas Perkins. Lean and elegant, with arresting dark eyes and a tempered steel mind, Gilman boasted an uncommon ability among most of her breed—she could laugh at herself.

This easy charm belied a turbulent past. Brought up in dire poverty after her father had abandoned the family, Charlotte Perkins married a successful young artist named Charles Stetson, then suffered a complete nervous breakdown following the birth of their daughter Katharine. Charlotte's precarious mental state became the focal point of her own scandalous divorce trial, and she lost all public sympathy after willingly giving up custody of her young daughter. While still battling the persistent aftereffects of her breakdown, Charlotte moved to California and began writing a feminist manifesto that called for women to abandon their traditional role as "a sex commodity." The book, *Women and Economics*, was published in 1898 and became a bestseller in seven languages. Two years later, Charlotte married New York attorney George Houghton Gilman, her first cousin and a relation of Kit's. That the groom was seven years younger than the bride further fanned the flames of controversy.

Now Charlotte Gilman, perhaps seeking to justify her controversial decision fifteen years earlier to entrust her daughter to the care of her ex-husband and his new wife, embarked on a campaign to liberate women from the "tyranny" of American motherhood. Instead of raising children in the home, Gilman advocated central nurseries run by professional care-givers. Only then, she explained, would women be free to seek work—and economic equality—outside the home. The concept of "day care" would not be popularized for another seventy years.

Kit, still finding it hard to imagine how women got along without cooks, maids, and nannies, applauded the idea the night Charlotte announced it at 133 Hawthorn. Dr. Hepburn changed the subject. For the rest of the evening, they traded stories about their mutual friend G. B. Shaw. (Diagnosed as suffering from breast cancer in 1932, Charlotte hoarded a supply of chloroform sufficient to prove fatal. After George Gilman's unexpected death two years later, she used the chloroform to end her life.)

Hartford-born Gilman's return to their midst was a bitter enough pill for the Hepburns' Republican neighbors to swallow, but it took the appearance on their doorstep that same evening of an anarchist powder-keg to really set off alarm bells at Nook Farm and throughout Hartford.

Emma Goldman was, as a biographer later put it, "born to ride whirlwinds." After fleeing an arranged marriage in her native Russia, Emma settled in New York City in 1889. There she met the fanatical revolutionary Alexander Berkman, and together they founded the radical monthly *Mother Earth*.

Listening to Goldman chatting amiably in Kit's Hartford salon, it would have been difficult to believe that this still-attractive woman with the upturned nose, flashing cobalt eyes, and exotic accent had plotted with Berkman to assassinate steel magnate Henry Clay Frick (Emma was not prosecuted, but Berkman spent fourteen years behind bars), served a year-long prison term for inciting to riot, narrowly escaped being implicated in the assassination of President William McKinley by the unbalanced anarchist Leon Czolgosz, and was stripped of her citizenship. ("Red Emma" would eventually serve another prison term, this time for opposing the draft, before being deported back to Russia in 1919. Alexander Berkman, despondent over his own ill health, committed suicide in 1936. Four years later, Emma Goldman, still officially labeled an "undesirable alien," died of a stroke. Remarkably, J. Edgar Hoover allowed her body to be returned to the United States for burial.)

Like Gilman and Hep, Emma was an ardent fan of George Bernard Shaw. In fact, the anarchist had quoted from his work so often in her firebrand speeches, Dame Rebecca West was moved to credit Goldman with popularizing Shaw in the United States.

The Norwegian playwright Henrik Ibsen was another of Goldman's favorites. It was Ibsen, Emma told her hosts, who confirmed what she already suspected from personal experience—that conventional, one-sided marriage was a "damnable lie" that chained women to the kitchen and left men free to roam. Not that she agreed with the holier-than-thou, antimale blandishments of the feminists. Emma felt profoundly that women could not "banish men out of their emotional life." There was only one solution, and Emma had coined a term for it: free love. Had Mrs. Bissell been asked to attend—and in the even more unlikely event she had accepted—Kit would now have been fetching the smelling salts.

Of all Kit's newfound radical friends, Pankhurst was

easily the closest, and Kit looked forward to having her visit once again in the fall of 1913. This time Pankhurst's visit would be for reasons of health as well as politics. After yet another prison stay in England and a prolonged hunger strike that had brought her to the brink of death, Pankhurst was released and ordered by her doctor to leave the country to recuperate.

When the French liner *La Provence* anchored in New York harbor, immigration authorities boarded the ship and reluctantly escorted Pankhurst to Ellis Island and its Board of Special Inquiry. Pankhurst's surprise detention was splashed across front pages around the world, and her sympathizers moved quickly. Mrs. O. H. P. Belmont, reigning queen of New York society, dispatched her lawyer to defend Pankhurst, but not even he was permitted to see her. "I went before these three men quite alone," Pankhurst would later tell Kit, "as many a poor, friendless woman without any of my resources had had to appear." The instant she entered the hearing room, Pankhurst spotted a complete dossier of her case in English legal papers. "These papers may have been supplied by Scotland Yard," she speculated. "They sufficed to convince the Board of Special Inquiry that I was a person of doubtful character, to say the least, and I was informed that I would have to be detained until the higher authorities in Washington examined my case." Two days later, Kit's old teacher at Bryn Mawr, President Woodrow Wilson, ordered her friend's release.

Kit was on the platform the evening Emmeline Pankhurst addressed thousands of supporters jamming Madison Square Garden. "Although you have a great deal of democracy there," Pankhurst began, "England is the most conservative country on earth. Why, your forefathers found that out a great many years ago! If you had passed your life in England as I have, you would know that there are certain words which aroused a feeling of horror and fear in the minds of the mass of the people. The word 'revolution,' for instance, was identified in England with all kinds of horrible ideas. The idea of change, the idea of unsettling the established order of things.

"Why, then, should not I come to ask for help for British women? Whatever helps them is going to help women all over the world. It will be the hastening of your victory. It has not been necessary in the United States for women to be militant in the sense that we are, and perhaps one of the reasons why it is not necessary and why it may never be necessary is that we are doing the militant work for you. And we are glad to do that work. We are *proud* to do that work. If there are any men who are fighters in this hall, any men who have taken part in warfare, I tell you, gentlemen, that amongst other good things you have kept from women, you have kept the joy of battle!"

She wound up with a quote from America's own Patrick Henry: " 'We have petitioned, we have demonstrated, we have supplicated, we have prostrated ourselves at the foot of the throne, and it has all been in vain. We must fight—I repeat it, sir, we must fight!' "

With that, the diminutive dynamo from Manchester sat down. Kit led the thundering ovation.

14.

What other people thought
didn't concern us much, anyway.
Most people are raised
to believe they are just as good
as the next person.
I was always told I was better.

Kit was making progress of a sort: Once looked upon by the neighbors merely as a misguided soul, she had now been promoted to the rank of dangerous radical. Kit handled the situation with typical aplomb, confronting the clucking society matrons with sweet-natured charm. "Whenever they snubbed her," says Kate, "she just kept smiling and saying hello until they finally caved in. Just kill 'em with kindness, that was her approach. They can't stay mad at you if you refuse to get mad back."

Still, Kathy and her siblings knew how it felt to be shunned. "Don't play with those Hepburn brats" was a common instruction, and Kathy understandably grew up with "a little bit of a chip on my shoulder."

Ostracism only served to draw the family closer, and that in turned fueled rumors about the goings-on inside the Hepburn household. Tom and Kathy, legend had it, were forced to watch the births of their siblings Dick (born in 1911), Bob (1913), Marion (1916), and Peggy (1918).

In truth, the Hepburn approach to raising children was anything but conventional. "At the dinner table," recalls Kate, "every conceivable topic was discussed—venereal disese, prostitution, feminism, Marxism, Darwinism, Fabianism, even nudism. I really had a rather leftist upbringing. But no bunk was tolerated."

All the Hepburn kids abided by a strict code of behavior laid down by Dad. Mind over matter was the order of the day. Chronic complaining was not tolerated. "If you weren't feeling well," says Kate, "nobody wanted to hear about it. We all feel sick every now and then, let's face it. But we were brought up as kids to please,

please go upstairs and keep it to yourself. Go to bed, go to sleep, or *something*—you were just supposed to stay out of sight until you felt better."

Ironically, discipline in the Hepburn house was probably more stringent than in other families. There was a reason: Kit and Hep were determined to maintain a united front against the onslaught of criticism. That meant no infighting. In the otherwise rambunctious, no-holds-barred atmosphere they had carefully cultivated at home, Kit and Hep fought about only one thing. "Never about money or any of those things husbands and wives are supposed to argue about," recalls Kate. "They only fought about politics. You didn't cross Mother on that topic." On a couple of occasions, Kit was angry enough to send crockery flying in Dad's direction—once, she hurled a full pot of hot coffee at him. "She was in a complete rage," recalls Kate. As for sibling rivalry: "It just didn't exist for us." The brother-sister battles common in other large families were kept to a bare minimum; quarreling was simply not allowed, and arguments among the kids were slapped down—literally—almost before they had a chance to begin.

At a time when the prevailing sentiment in polite society was anticorporal punishment, Kathy was unabashedly proud of having a "spanking dad." Recalls Kate: "Were we spanked? *Beaten*."

Dr. Hepburn seemed to relish his reputation as a disciplinarian, and Kate remembers in vivid detail one occasion when he made a special effort to live up to that reputation. "Our cousins and most of the other children were never punished. Our house was always full of children and nurses and visitors in the summer—Aunt

Edith had five children, Aunt Marion had three—and when we got together to eat we had to push two huge tables together. So one day, I knocked over a glass of milk onto the table and began laughing hysterically— don't ask me why. Dad stood up and said, 'Come upstairs.'

"Everyone just sat there looking on in *horror*. Absolute terror. And we went upstairs to my bedroom, and Dad grabbed a tennis racket out of the closet and started whacking a pillow while I screamed bloody murder." When they came back downstairs, the guests were ashen. Finally Edith spoke up, blasting Hep for what, in her view, amounted to child abuse. "Everybody was so upset they almost stormed out of the house in a fury. Dad just let them rant on and on while I sat there looking stricken—God, it was funny. Daddy was strict, all right, but he couldn't pass up a good laugh. We filled them in on what really happened later, though I don't think it struck them as all that amusing."

Dad's anger was the genuine article when he summoned all six Hepburn children into his study after dinner one night to deliver an ultimatum. The kids had been using his bottom dresser drawer to stow away their treasures—turtles and rocks and pocket knives—among his sweaters and his underwear, and this had to stop. He ordered them to remove the items and to never, ever use his drawer as a hiding place again. If one failed to obey, *all* would be punished. End of subject. Now go.

None of the children had seen their father so angry, and each figured the others would be scared off. "When Dad opened the drawer the next day, he found *even more*

---

things tucked away among his clothes. When he realized what had happened, Daddy thought it was hilarious—and we were relieved."

From the beginning Hep was, in spite of his busy schedule, a strong presence in the lives of all the children. It is interesting that, aside from her clear memories of her mother's intense activism, Dad is central in most of Kathy's early memories.

It was Hep, for instance, who had Hartford's Pope Manufacturing Company design and build a special bicycle for his daughter equipped with what would later be called training wheels. He then placed Kathy on it atop a hill, and gave her a healthy shove. Kathy was three and "paralyzed with fear, holding on to the handle bars for dear life. I could see a little old man walking along the street, down at the bottom of the hill. He was like a magnet; I headed straight for him. I was certain we'd crash, but he just smiled and caught me when I reached the bottom. I'd made it alive!"

From about the same time, she remembers the morning bathing ritual that started with a plunge in a tub of ice water, then a dash to the fireplace where Kit would wrap her in a red Indian blanket. "The cold baths were Dad's idea, though Mother rather believed in it, too," says Kate, who has made a lifelong habit of taking several frigid showers *a day* to ward off colds. "You see, Dad was a great believer in a change of temperature. I take a hot shower, then I stand in ice water every morning until I'm absolutely frozen." This notion that "It's no good for you if it doesn't make you suffer" has also prompted Kate to keep swimming in the waters off her Connecticut home on Long Island Sound throughout the winter and to coax her friends to follow her into the icy water. "I swim all winter, but that wasn't Dad's idea—he didn't take it that far," she now admits. "And he'd never think of making other people do it. He was more noble. I do it just to see if I can make myself do something as unpleasant as that and still survive. Incidentally, I don't force anyone else to do it. They see me and they feel the cowardice in their own behavior. I shame them into it."

After her father, Tom Jr. was the male figure Kathy admired most. Brother and sister had stood up together against the ostracism of the neighbors, and now illness drew them even closer. At age five, Tom was stricken with St. Vitus's dance, also known as chorea. The nervous disorder left him with a discernable facial twitch which would disappear within a few years, but in the meantime he was teased mercilessly by his classmates at Hartford's public West Middle School—so much so that he found it impossible to concentrate, and his grades began to slip. Tom was temporarily removed from the school to recover, and a tutor was hired.

At about the same time, Kathy fell seriously ill. "I came down with scarlet fever," she recalls. "Now *that* was dangerous. Affected my ears. Abscess. Terrible. Painful." But she recovered quickly enough to show up a neighbor lady who had the audacity to call her "frail." Says Kate: "I'm not sure I remember it, but Mother told me that I headed straight for a big oak. Ran right into it full force. Showed her."

Kit and Hep did nothing to discourage their daughter's fierce streak of independence. Not surprisingly, Kathy turned into the ultimate tomboy. "I was," Kate says without a trace of undue modesty, "a wonderful athlete. I could outdive, outswim, and outrun anybody. I could do anything on a bicycle. I could walk on my hands." Dr. Hepburn ran a rope from the front corner of the front yard at an angle all the way to the back. "A rope ladder led up to a flying trapeze that was about thirty feet in the air, and I used to slide down the whole length of the lawn to the ground." Using another rope that dangled from the bar, Kathy would pull the trapeze back and start again. "My favorite thing was just to hang by my toes above the gravel path, and my mother told me years after that she used to watch me and think, 'What are we going to do if she falls off?' I never did."

As a passionate tree-climber, Kathy loved to "shinny up a birch, then, once I got to the top, throw my weight off it so that I'd whip around." She was careful not to be catapulted into the neighbors' yard. "Christ, no—I never let go! I would have been killed! The whole point was to hang on for dear life."

When she was in a more reflective mood, Kathy would climb up to the top of the hemlock tree that stood on the edge of the front lawn and "sit there happily for hours, watching people go by." If she felt sociable, Kathy waved to Laurel Avenue's Irish cop on the beat, Officer Keefe. "Neighbors would call up and say 'Kathy's sitting in the top of the tree,' and Mother would say, 'Well for heaven's sake, don't frighten her.' "

Nothing could frighten her. In the winter months the pulley and the trapeze were taken down, and the circular drive, now banked with ten-foot-high walls of snow, was transformed into a feudal ice fortress where Kathy and her brother Tom bravely held off snowball-armed invaders.

At 5 P.M. on these snowy days, the call would go out among the Nook Farm kids that Dr. Hepburn's battered, doorless old Maxwell with the license plates reading 3405 had been spotted by a lookout. With Kathy leading the pack, the kids would run after the car, toss a sled rope over the convertible's rear bumper, and "hang on the ride." Dr. Hepburn did not slow down—in fact, there remains a lingering suspicion that with one eye on the rearview mirror he actually speeded up as he rounded the final corner home. Kathy, applauded by the factory workers and Officer Keefe, usually ended her wild ride by careening headlong into a snowdrift.

Even when there was no snow on the ground, Dr. Hepburn willingly played the role of Pied Piper. As soon as he came home and finished his cup of tea, the cry "3-4-0-5" went up, and practically every kid in the neighborhood rushed to the abandoned tennis court to roughhouse in games organized by Dr. Hepburn.

In choosing games, Hep saw to it that democracy ruled. "If the general vote was, for instance, between prisoner's base (the precursor of tag) and baseball, baseball always won. But I was an absolute whiz at prisoner's base, and I much preferred it. And on my birthday the vote was to play baseball, and I said 'That's a rotten thing to do.' My father said, 'That's the majority vote.' I said, 'But it's my *birthday*.' He said that didn't matter. I was in a fury. An absolute fury. I thought it was very unjust." There may have been other reasons for the doctor's intractability. "I suppose," Kate concedes, "he would rather have played baseball. But I didn't like the game then—and I don't now."

Kathy and Tom remained inseparable in play—and in school. Every morning from the age of four, Kathy walked with her brother to West Middle School—east on Hawthorn Street, down Laurel, and across Farmington to Niles. Boasting an imposing colonial facade, West Middle, like many public schools constructed around the turn of the century, more closely resembled a scaled-down replica of Philadelphia's Independence Hall than a public elementary school. Situated among the stately homes of Hartford, however, West Middle seemed perfectly suited to its manicured surroundings.

On the way home from school, Kathy and Tom would stop at Childs' drug store to indulge their mutual sweet tooth with licorice, button candy, and Hersey's chocolate. At Murphy's grocery store, the fare ran to Fig Newtons and Toll House cookies. "Sweets are my downfall—Baker's chocolate, right out of the box," Kate would tell me seven decades later. "And ice cream—I could sit down right now and eat a quart of maple walnut. No problem. You see, that's what happens when you get started early."

Tom couldn't always keep a watchful eye on his little sister. Late one afternoon, shortly after her fourth birthday, Kathy tagged along when Kit went Christmas shopping. Kathy got lost in the crush of shoppers, and after searching for her mother for a half-hour, the little girl calmly walked outside and asked a woman getting into her Model A Ford if she'd give her a lift home. The child seemed sure enough of herself, so the woman obliged. A block short of her address, however, Kathy asked the woman to let her off. "You needn't go any farther," she said, and added cryptically, "Everyone in that house only speaks French."

The Hepburns' nanny, Fanny Ciarrier (later Anglicized to "Carrier"), did indeed speak French; Kit and Dr. Hepburn paid her way to the United States with her son John Marcel, who grew up with the Hepburn children. Fanny (who continued working for the Hepburns until her death forty-two years later) was stocky, dark-haired, apple-cheeked, smelled of lavender, and had a temper. She was, above all else, deeply fond of the children.

When Kathy strolled into the kitchen alone, Fanny asked her where her mother had gone. "Oh, she's still downtown shopping," Kathy replied. "But don't worry. A nice lady brought me home. I'll put myself to bed."

Back at the store, Kit was in a panic. Not wanting to upset Fanny, Mrs. Hepburn called home and asked to speak to the doctor. Hep was not home yet, and when Kit got him at the office, she told him that she couldn't find Kathy. They were frantic but agreed that at all costs they should spare Fanny the horrible truth of Kathy's disappearance. While Kit combed Hartford, Dr. Hepburn kept calling home to ask if Kit had returned. After a dozen calls, an exasperated Fanny finally told the doctor that there was nobody home but Tom and Kathy— and that Kathy had been asleep upstairs for over an hour.

15.

Being a girl was a torment.

The Pequot Indians were the first to summer there, fishing and swimming off this narrow sandspit where the Connecticut River flows into the open sea. In the early seventeenth century, Lady Alice Butler gave up her privileged noblewoman's life in England to join her husband, Col. George Fenwick, in the colonies. Fenwick had been appointed governor of the town of Saybrook on the Connecticut shore. Lady Fenwick died in 1648, and was buried on what would be the site of the old Saybrook Fort.

Fenwick, as the half-mile-wide peninsula off Old Saybrook would be called, remained a marshy, windswept paradise populated by only a few hardy fishermen and lighthouse keepers—until the completion of the Connecticut Valley Railroad in 1871 linked Hartford to the coast. (Ironically, Lady Alice Fenwick's body was disinterred to make way for the construction of a railroad roundhouse on the sight of the old fort. A crowd of local folk showed up for a glimpse of her ladyship's 237-year-old remains, and as soon as she was disinterred some even snipped off locks of her famous auburn hair for souvenirs.)

That same year, Fenwick Hall, a huge resort hotel billed as "one of the finest on the Atlantic coast," opened its doors to wealthy and influential guests from all over the Northeast. One of them was Tammany Hall boss Edward R. Stokes, who had gained some considerable notoriety in 1869 when he shot and killed railroad tycoon "Jubilee Jim" Fiske in a duel over a young woman. Stokes was never prosecuted for this "crime of passion." When mismanagement forced Fenwick Hall into bankruptcy, Stokes sailed his black-hulled yacht *Fra Diavolo* (translation: "Brother Devil") up from New York to buy the hotel at auction. Stokes's only competition was a Roman Catholic bishop who wanted to turn Fenwick Hall into an orphanage. Several hours before the bidding was to begin, Stokes invited the good bishop out for a sail to sample the cuisine prepared by his new chef Oscar (who went on to make quite a name for himself as Oscar of the Waldorf). Once *Fra Diavolo* was several miles offshore, the yacht stopped dead in the water. Engine trouble, the skipper said. By the time the ship did make it back to Fenwick, the auction had already been held, and Stokes's representatives—facing no competition from the Bishop—had picked Fenwick Hall up for a bargain-basement price.

Under Stokes, Fenwick Hall became a favorite gathering place for politicos, Wall Street financiers, and entertainers. But within a few years Stokes, whose no-expense-spared approach extended to breeding his own terrapin for his guests' turtle soup, was forced to sell. The buyer was no less a character himself, though a typically Hartford one.

Morgan Gardner Bulkeley's family founded the Aetna Life Insurance Company in 1853. Bulkeley himself was Hartford's mayor, then Connecticut's governor, and capped his political career as a United States senator. The Brainards, who helped the Bulkeleys run the Aetna, soon followed, and on their heels came the rest of Hartford's moneyed elite. In 1899, Bulkeley's Hartford gang made the final break with the mainland, establishing Fenwick as a self-governing borough within Old Saybrook.

After four sweltering summers in the city, the Hepburns began to cast about in the spring of 1912 for a seaside retreat of their own. Kit's suffragette ally Josephine "Jo" Day Bennett had invited them up to Fenwick to stay at her family's sprawling "cottage," and they were smitten by the peace and the charm of the tight-knit little borough. There was no way Hep could afford to buy one of these pricey homes alone. But when George Roberts, a Congregationalist minister and heir to the Hartford Carpet Company fortune, put his Fenwick house up for sale, Hep wasted no time in persuading his brother-in-law Donald Hooker to go in with him on the deal.

The Hepburn cottage was a sprawling, three-story affair—all weathered shingles, brick chimneys (there were three), and creaking floorboards. Hard by the Sound at Fenwick's northeastern tip—wooden steps led from the backyard directly down to the rocky beach— and separated from the community by a grassy marsh, the house mirrored the family's standing at Fenwick: just a little bit apart. The Hepburn cottage, with its unobstructed view of two lighthouses and the mouth of the Connecticut River, had another unusual feature: it was standing on a sandbar. (Amazingly, the structure would weather several violent storms before a hurricane struck in 1938, forcing Kit and her movie-star daughter to flee the house before it was destroyed. Using toy blocks purchased from F. A. O. Schwartz in New York, they sat on the floor of the West Hartford house and planned out what the new cottage would look like. After several pitched battles about just what configuration the new Fenwick house would take, it was rebuilt—on the same spot—in 1939.)

The day they moved in, the Hepburns received their first guest—none other than Fenwick's most distinguished citizen, Morgan Gardner Bulkeley. Bulkeley, whose wife Fannie Houghton was a distant cousin of Kit's, welcomed Hep with a smile, then presented him with a bill for $500—his share of what it cost to maintain the wooden bulkhead that ran behind his house and along much of the Fenwick shore.

Fenwick was a child's summer dream, especially for the Hepburn tomboy. Its glorious physical pleasures allayed her sense of childhood as "a torment"—a period of her life when, she says, "from the age of nine to age thirteen, I shaved my head. I told everyone it was to keep cool, but I really did it so the boys couldn't grab hold of my hair when we wrestled. I called myself 'Jimmy.' " And so at Fenwick, "Jimmy," her hair shorn, wearing knee-length cotton knickers with one of her brother's shirts, dug clams, swam, dived off piers, rode her bicycle, and gathered up shells, driftwood, and sharks' teeth. She raced the other kids down the beach and beat them all—except for Tom, now fully recovered from chorea and the star athlete of the family. Tom, she recalls, "won so many ribbons for running at the annual Fenwick track meet that they finally had to put a limit on the number you could win."

The Hepburn cottage at Fenwick, like the house at 133 Hawthorn, became a sort of general headquarters for local youngsters. While their parents played golf, tennis, or bridge, the children raced in and out of the kitchen, where the icebox was open to all comers. There was a third-floor attic riddled with scary secret passageways, and a hammock on the wide porch where Kit managed to nap undisturbed while a dozen kids clomped about. "Beneath the porch," Kate remembers, "there were rope swings where my cousins and I would try to knock each other off. Mayhem. Mother slept through it all."

Another mecca for Kathy and the other kids was the old bathhouse next to the Fenwick Pier, a domed pavilion where children could set up lemonade stands—locals recall several price-slashing wars—or ride their bicycles round and round on the wooden floor when it rained.

Like most small New England towns, Fenwick prided itself on its patriotism—and, more specifically, on its pull-out-the-stops Fourth of July celebrations. Red, white, and blue bunting adorned the bathhouse, where town fathers reviewed a parade led by a firetruck festooned with flags. Sousa marches boomed. Chests swelled. And everyone waited for the grand finale: Fenwick's famous fireworks display.

Parents, fearing that little Johnny might blow off a finger or blind himself, forbade all children from setting off firecrackers on their own (of course many, including the headstrong Kathy, still did anyway). Instead they chipped in to hire professionals to do the job, and each year crowds gathered on the beach to watch the rockets fire out over the Sound and explode in a blaze of color.

On one July Fourth, a pyrotechnic "expert" hired by the good people of Fenwick stumbled and dropped a burning cigarette into a box of fireworks. In an instant, Kate Hepburn's sister Marion would recall, "Fenwick's waterfront was a holocaust of flames and deafening explosions. Parents and children fled for cover. Old

Grandmother Moore and her chauffeur were sitting in her automobile when a rocket whizzed through the open windows of the car, singeing off some of her hair! A young couple happened to be sitting in a wicker swing on a front porch, peacefully holding hands and watching the show. To their horror, a fiery rocket swooshed right past them into the living room. Fortunately the rocket failed to explode." No one was injured, though from then on there would be no more fireworks displays. Fittingly, Fenwick's annual tradition had gone out with a bang.

The closest thing to "pure excitement" for Kathy was sailing her "sneak box," a small, precariously balanced boat that she proudly christened *Tiger* by smashing a bottle of root beer over its bow. Since sneak boxes had a tendency to capsize, they were restricted to the shallow South Cove, where even young sailors could wade to safety.

One August afternoon, Kathy decided to ignore the threatening storm clouds and take her brother Tom on a cruise—just to show him what a deft skipper she had become. The seas turned choppy, and while Tom and Kathy struggled to keep the boat upright they were swept three miles down the coast—and out toward the open sea.

Fisherman Frank Ingham was steaming home with his catch when he spotted the castaways. As the seas grew rougher, he pulled the kids onto his boat and headed for shore. Later, all that was left of Kathy's sneak box— a board bearing the name *Tiger*—washed up on the beach.

No matter. Her rough-hewn, lanky rescuer wore a

tweed cap, rolled-up sleeves, and hip boots. A pipe was clenched in his teeth, and he threw back his head when he laughed. Kathy was smitten. Ingham's fish shed, just a few hundred yards east of the Hepburn cottage, became Kathy's special place, where she learned how to clean and fillet fish. Ingham, recognizing a special spark in the feisty little girl who called herself "Jimmy," also taught her how to row a whaler against the tide. Kathy was inspired to fantasize about herself as a Pearl White-type heroine named "Grace Darling," pulling shipwrecked sailors from a raging surf.

Kathy's magical world was threatened when the establishment at Fenwick, viewing Ingham's fish shed as a commercial eyesore, ordered him to shut it down. Kathy begged her father to help, and he put Ingham in touch with one of Hartford's top attorneys. The battle raged for seven years before Ingham lost and was forced off the beach and out of the fishing business. He then began cutting and selling ice, and Kathy remained so steadfastly loyal that after the cottage was rebuilt in 1939, the world-acclaimed actress insisted that an icebox be installed next to the refrigerator—just so Ingham could keep making his deliveries.

Ingham was only one of the adults who populated Kathy's world at Fenwick and whose influence on her would last a lifetime. There was Mary Towle, one of Mother's confederates from Bryn Mawr and her fellow "innocent abroad" on the now legendary European spree. "Aunty" Towle, who had become a distinguished attorney practicing in New York, was one of Kathy's favorites—despite the fact that she, unlike the Hepburns, attended church regularly. "We were not religious in the traditional sense," says Kate, "not at all. Didn't go to church." But when Grandfather Hepburn came to Fenwick, he always preached at St. Mary's-by-the-Sea, and "all of us sinners" went to hear him.

The Reverend Hepburn, who had long since stopped trying to convince his son to return to religion, was a master storyteller. Even more than his spellbinding sermons, Pastor Hep's fairytales—told in a voice resonant with the hickory-sweet sounds of Virginia and his Missouri boyhood—mesmerized Kathy and in all likelihood gave her a gentle first nudge in the direction of acting. "We used to wait for my grandfather to come and tell us stories," she recalls. "He had this fantastic *way* of wrapping you up in this fantasy world. He had a particularly wonderful version of *The Musicians of Bremen*. It was my favorite." (Beginning sometime in his late fifties, the reverend developed a tremor of the hands that got progressively worse. His solution: a couple of stiff belts. "Grandfather Hepburn drank whiskey to control the shakes," Kate recalled some seventy years after her childhood summers, when she found herself coping with the same inherited disorder. "It works," she reported, "if you drink enough.")

Kit did not allow the delightful and relaxed summers at Fenwick to become vacations from her causes—much to her husband's dismay. One evening, after making the grueling six-hour drive from Hartford to Fenwick for the weekend, he arrived only to find the cottage crowded with suffragettes. Kit's old comrade-in-arms Emily Pierson took one look at the scowling Dr. Hepburn and quipped, "Well, Hep, whose cottage do you think this is, anyway?" With that, he took the startled woman by the arm, out the front door, and led her straight to her car. By the time he returned to escort the next interloper out, the ladies were gathering up their coats and hurriedly bidding Kit goodbye.

"Any doubts, dear?" Dr. Hepburn asked his wife.

"None, dear," she replied with a smile, pouring him a cup of tea. "Care for some cinnamon toast?"

16.

Mother knew things
don't happen unless you
make them happen.

There was no one to greet Detective Pigniuolo when he stepped onto the platform at the Hartford train station a few days before Christmas 1912, and that's just the way Pigniuolo wanted it. He had been hired by the United States government to track down a character named Fusco—just Fusco—who was reputed to be the biggest trafficker in prostitution on the eastern seaboard.

Even the streetwise Pigniuolo was stunned to discover Fusco's brothel thriving in the middle of the city, just two blocks away from police headquarters on land owned by the Catholic Church. Pigniuolo also learned that the tenements housing Fusco's other nefarious operations were owned by some of Hartford's finest families.

Pigniuolo was closing in on his prey when, without warning, he was arrested by the local police. Fusco had gotten word of the detective's investigation and neatly turned the tables, accusing Pigniuolo of blackmail. "When I read this in the paper," Kit would recall two years later in a speech before the National Association of College Alumnae, "it seemed to me that it was just the sort of trial at which women ought to be present. They were talking about the buying and selling of women, and if women were concerned about any questions they were concerned about this. So I went down to the trial. There were no other women there."

The only woman at the trial could not believe what she was hearing. "Sergeant Hart, chief of our detective bureau, was on the stand. The attorney for Pigniuolo was cross-examining him. It went something like this:

" 'You knew that Fusco conducted a house of ill fame, did you not?'

147

" 'Yes.'

" 'Did you ever make a complaint?'

" 'No, I didn't see why I should. The house was established before I went on the beat and I saw no reason why I should make a complaint.'

" 'If you went on your beat at twelve o'clock and a burglary that had been started before that time was in process of operation, would you consider it your duty to arrest the burglar?'

" 'Of course.'

" 'If you knew that an established house was running openly within the shadow of the police station ruining girls' souls and bodies would you consider it your duty to make a complaint?'

" 'No.'

"That was the attitude of the chief of the detective force of our city."

The trial yielded other sobering revelations. In the course of a single year, Fusco had imported 135 girls—many as young as seventeen—from New York City to "apprentice" in Hartford. Fusco complained that the newly passed Mann Act against transporting women across state lines for immoral purposes meant that he'd have to stop bringing in girls from New York. But he was not concerned. "I can get plenty," he said with a shrug, "here in Connecticut."

Pigniuolo was acquitted, but to Kit's amazement Fusco was not indicted. "After the trial," recounted Kit, "the labor unions passed resolutions condemning the previous policy of our city. The Federation of Churches passed resolutions. The mayor closed the houses, and in a short time people began saying, 'They will open up again in a little while. It was just like this two years ago and everything opened up again as soon as things quieted down.' "

This time, it was only a matter of weeks before the house reopened. Kit sprang into action. Box camera in hand, she marched down to Fusco's house and began snapping away. Out front, dozens of neighborhood children smiled for Kit's camera.

Inside, several of the girls guilelessly took her on a tour of the premises. The rooms reserved for customers were reasonably clean, but Kit was not prepared for the squalid conditions under which the prostitutes themselves were forced to live, some with small children. When one of the women showed her an open toilet into which a prostitute's toddler had fallen and drowned, Kit did not cry; she recorded it on film.

Hoping to stir public consciousness, Kit sent her photograph to the *Courant* and they published it. "This all happened during a big community event called 'Made in Hartford Week,' " explains Kate. When the *Courant*'s editor, Kit's old nemesis Charles Hopkins Clark, saw the picture he hit the roof, but it was too late. "Of course, they yanked the picture after the first edition, but Mother had made her point," Kate says proudly. "She really was a hothead."

Nevertheless, progress was nil. "We waited," recalled Kit. "Apparently nothing was going to be done." So, once again, Kit took it upon herself to act. She invited some of the nation's top experts on prostitution and venereal disease to speak at a public forum. Kit's critics did not bother to wait for the meeting itself. They tried instead to fight back by attacking the posters that had been printed up for the forum showing a woman and her young daughter looking at a sign which read "DANGER! Mothers Beware! Sixty Thousand Innocent Girls Wanted to Take the Place of Sixty Thousand White Slaves Who Will Die This Year In the U.S."

"This picture shocked the *Hartford Times* and other papers," Kit said. "It was not the conditions that shocked them, strange to say, but the fact that we were determined to speak of these conditions. They protested that these circulars were being distributed where women could see them, and we replied that women were the very ones for whom they were intended!"

It was another full house at the Parsons Theatre. A last-minute phone call from the mayor threatening to revoke the theater's license on grounds of indecency failed to halt the meeting. Inside the hall, forty volunteer ushers lined the aisles, dressed in white and wearing blue-and-silver ribbons proclaiming "Knowledge Is Power."

The theater fell silent as Kit spoke of Fusco's brothel, of the child who drowned in the open toilet, and of the corrupt city administration that was allowing all this to continue. If the white slavers were ever to be thrown out of Hartford, Kit told them, women would be the ones to do it.

"The reason for this is not that women are good and men are bad," Kit told her audience. "It is because through all the ages women have been bearing the burden of social evil. We have been reaping the wild oats that men have sown—from the prostitute to the girl with an illegitimate child to the wife with a hidden disease she dare not even mention. It is one of the most striking

150

facts of modern times that although for the first time in the history of the human race thousands of girls of tender age are working in factories and shops, even low wages and long hours cannot drive enough women into the life to supply the demand for prostitutes.

"Women have been trained to a sense of responsibility in regard to sex which men have never had. That is one of the great things that men have done for us. Men have said to us, 'If we are going to take you into our homes and make you the mothers of our children then you must prove that you are fit for motherhood. You must bring a clean record.' They have made this one demand of us so uncompromisingly that the very term virtue as applied to women has come to mean virtue in regard to sex.

"Women," Kit went on, "have not been in a position to make demands of men. Until recent years men have owned even our property and our children—our *legitimate* children, that is; women have always been allowed to own their illegitimate children, of course. Men have had all the education, all of the control—financial, social, and political. Women have not been in a position to make any demands of men at all. When we are in a position to make demands—and we will be someday— I believe that the first demand we shall make of men will be the demand that men have made of us. And when that time comes, I believe that men will have gained as much as women. For every man, even the worst, knows in his heart that the present state of affairs is *wrong*."

The next day, at the downtown offices of the Connecticut Woman Suffrage Association, Kit was besieged with offers of support. "Old and young, rich and poor came in," she would later tell the National Association of College Women. Even antisuffrage leaders—the "Antis" who had been slandering her for years—came to sign up for Kit's campaign to clean up the city. "Antis drove up in limousines—for Antis always ride in limousines in our town. They came in and said, 'I don't want to vote, but I am with you in this, I can tell you.' It seemed odd that they would approve of this when they thought voting unladylike. What we were doing was so much more unladylike than voting could ever possibly be!"

Soon Kit and her troops hit the streets, plastering signs in store windows and on telephone poles listing the names of the twenty-four elected city officials of both parties—from the mayor on down—who had allowed the whorehouses to stay in operation. "Without the vote," Kit said, "we had little pressure to bring to bear, so we thought we'd try a little domestic pressure. The wives and daughters of these twenty-four men, as well as their neighbors, were sure to see our signs."

The tactic worked. Fusco's whorehouses were closed for good, ending Hartford's ignominious reign as the white-slave capital of the East.

17.

I really wanted to be a surgeon, like Dad. But fairytales were a big piece of my life, and I was such a *good* fairytale-teller.

Kathy stood on the deck of the boat as it pitched from side to side, her broad, pink face turned up to the sky. She did not mind the bone-chilling wind that swept up off New York Harbor, nor the bitter sting of the sea spray. In fact, she rather enjoyed the feeling.

As the boat drew closer to Liberty Island, the Lady of the Harbor loomed larger and larger, until she seemed to fill the horizon. "Magnificent, eh, Redtop?" said Dad. But Kathy was momentarily preoccupied; she seemed more fascinated by the sight of the crewmembers leaping from the deck and scrambling frantically to tie the boat to the oil-blackened pilings.

Dr. Hepburn grasped his little girl's hand and led her into the statue. An elevator manufactured by a new Hartford company called Otis carried them up into the crown where Dad lifted Kathy up to one of the windows. Perched on a polished brass railing, Kathy gazed in wonder at the jagged skyline dominated by the world's tallest structure, the sixty-story Woolworth Building. On this overcast afternoon, the Brooklyn Bridge looked like a pretty necklace of sparkling lights strung over the East River. Dozens of liners steamed into port—toy boats in a bathtub.

"Feel like a good climb, Redtop?" Off to the side was a doorway. Kathy went first, Dr. Hepburn right behind her—up, up, up a spiral staircase until they emerged in a crystal bubble, inside the flame of the torch of the Statue of Liberty. "Thrilling. Exhilarating. Magical. If you've ever been lucky enough to get up there," Kate would say a lifetime later, "you never forget it."

In the spring of 1917 the Hepburns moved out of their

now-cramped quarters on Hawthorn Street into a bigger if decidedly less eccentric house right around the corner, at 352 Laurel. The United States had entered the Great War in Europe on the side of the allies, and the nation was gearing up to join the holy crusade against the kaiser. The Hepburns were barely touched by the conflict. Their own sons were too young to fight, and their contemporaries were too old. Hep, like the rest of the staff at Hartford Hospital, did volunteer to treat veterans free of charge, and Kit pitched in to sell war bonds. But their energies were still focused on the social crusades they had been championing for nearly a decade. The battles they chose to fight, for the most part, remained close to home.

On the suffrage front, Kit once again found herself fighting more conservative elements within the movement itself. The National American Woman Suffrage Association, of which the Connecticut association was now a member, had decided on a state-by-state approach rather than an attack on the federal level. Kit railed against this strategy as unnecessarily time-consuming, but to no avail.

Kit became bitterly disappointed in the national leadership, and she was not alone. A more militant faction led by Alice Paul had broken away to form the Woman's Party, and Kit was ready to join them. On September 17, 1917, she stepped down as president of the organization she had founded. In seven years, it had grown to include more than one hundred branches and thirty-eight thousand members.

"I have come to have a very deep personal affection for the members of the board," she wrote in her letter of resignation. "It is a great grief to me to realize that if I am to follow my honest convictions I must sever my official relations with you.

"I have reluctantly come to feel that the policy of the National Association in their work for the federal amendment is futile, academic, and out of date. After the last National Convention, held in Atlantic City, I felt pretty hopeless about the ability of the National Association to lead us to victory.

"The National Woman Suffrage Association is not the only national association working for woman suffrage. The Woman's Party, a younger and more vigorous body, is devoting all its energies to securing the passage of the federal amendment. Today, more than ever, the importance of woman suffrage is thrown into high relief. England, Russia, and Canada have given women the vote since the war began. With their men gone it is imperative for the women left at home, the only representatives of their families, to have a voice in the government. Both industrially and politically women in wartime do the work of the men who have gone to the front.

"We have gone to war for democracy and yet millions of women in our own country are denied the right to vote. Simply mentioning this fact in suffrage journals and to suffrage audiences is futile. We must say it in such a way that all the world will hear, and that is what the pickets of the Woman's Party have done at Washington. My sympathies are all with them. I admire their honesty, their selflessness, and their practical wisdom. It is through these women that we shall secure the suffrage." Kit then exhorted her fellow suffragists to "Support the Woman's Party!"

Meantime, at West Middle School, ten-year-old Kathy was testing the patience of her teachers. Her best friend in the fifth grade was Florence Miel, a pretty, curly-haired minister's daughter. Kathy, with her close-cropped hair and wiry frame, was in awe of Florence's soft femininity, though the two shared a mischievous streak.

The girls' teacher was Miss Lynes, a large, severe-looking woman whose looks belied a kind disposition. Kathy was Miss Lynes's star pupil in arithmetic, and Miss Lynes was easily the nicest teacher Kathy had ever had. One day shortly after noon, while the teachers were eating lunch in their second-floor cafeteria, the two girls dashed in shouting, "Old Lady Lynes. Old Lady Lynes." Hurtful behavior. Miss Lynes may have been all of thirty.

The next day, Kit ordered Kathy to lug a heavy potted geranium all the way to school and give it to Miss Lynes "as an admission of my guilt and an indication of my sorrow. Miss Lynes put it on her desk. It was there humiliating me for weeks." (Eventually all was forgiven, and "Old Lady Lynes" remained a friend of Kathy's even after her unpredictable pupil became one of Hollywood's brightest stars).

A more constant source of humiliation for Kathy was her freckles. "Mother had some, and Dad did, but I was the only one absolutely *covered* with them. I remember listening to all the talk about nudity and false modesty and thinking to myself, someday, nobody is going to wear any clothes. The only thing that bothered me was that I was totally freckled from head to foot, and nobody would want me. So I confided this fear to my father, and he said, 'I want to tell you something, Kathy, and you must never forget it. Jesus Christ, Alexander the Great, and Leonardo da Vinci all had red hair and freckles, and they did all right.' "

A few years later, Kathy would show that she had taken her father's words to heart. While attending Hartford's Oxford School, she took a class in horseback riding. The students' horses were rented from Sergeant Anniger's stables at the Troop B Armory on Farmington Avenue "just past Quaker Lane." When the time came to choose a horse, Kathy didn't hesitate. She rushed up to a pony named Leopard and threw her arms around his neck. "I'll take him," she yelled, "he's perfect. We both have speckles!" (One day she would similarly explain her affection for her fellow "speckled" humans: "I think people with freckles are sort of sweet and pathetic, like some lovable family pet.")

It was about this time, around the age of ten, that Kathy was bitten by the drama bug. She had, after all, been a supporting player during Kit's social campaigns, waving placards and selling balloons stenciled *Votes for Women*. And then there were Grandpa Hepburn's magical tales of princesses and trolls that had fired her imagination. It was not true, as later Hepburn mythology would have it, that Dr. Hepburn constructed a tot-sized proscenium theater behind the Laurel Street house so that his daughter might pursue her art; on the contrary, he would have thought such an indulgence a frivolous waste of time, even for a child.

There was, however, a dilapidated garden shed out back where the Hepburns stored their helmets, basketballs, croquet mallets, rackets, and other athletic equipment. It was here that Kathy built her own miniature stage. "I used to do a lot of plays," she says, "where I moved cardboard figures around and told them what to say. We had a woman who used to come in on Thursdays—all day Thursday—to sew, and I used to do shows for her. Her name was Mary Ryan, and she seemed to appreciate the entertainment. Well, she tolerated it." One of the first Hepburn roles: the part of Topsy in *Uncle Tom's Cabin*. "Eva was too goody-goody for my taste, so I let some poor soul play her."

Taking her new thespian impulse to Fenwick, Kathy found willing confederates in her brothers. At Mother's invitation Bishop Howden, a visiting clergyman from Santa Fe, New Mexico, took advantage of his sermon at St. Mary's-by-the-Sea to make an appeal for his impoverished Navajo parishioners. To raise funds for children of the Navajo, Kathy charged the Hepburns' Fenwick neighbors fifty cents admission to see her backyard production of *Beauty and the Beast*. With the help of younger brothers Dick and Bob, a stage was jerry-rigged out of cardboard boxes and orange crates. Tom provided musical accompaniment, strumming along on a banjo. "My friend Allie Barbour played the beauty; I played the beast," says Kate. "I got done up in a white flannel donkey's head and a Little Lord Fauntleroy suit that was royal blue velvet with a strip of silver tape around the cape—very glamorous. Why a donkey's head, I don't know. But I looked beastly enough."

The play raised almost seventy dollars, but Kathy was livid when she eventually learned that the Indians spent the cash on a new Victrola with, it was alleged, the biggest trumpet in the Southwest. Still, *Beauty and the Beast* was enough of a box-office and critical success ("Nobody walked out, anyway") for Kathy to tackle next the chain-rattling part of Marley's Ghost in Dickens's *A Christmas Carol*.

"It is a complete mystery to me why I had this urge to go out and display myself," muses Kate. "I was and am basically a very, very shy person. Most actors are. Daddy used to say I wouldn't go to parties because I was afraid I wouldn't be either the bride or the corpse. That I wouldn't, in other words, be the center of attention. The *star*. Shyness really is just self-consciousness taken to an extreme degree. The minute you walk into a room, you're always sort of asking 'So—how'm I doing?' We actors are all egocentrics."

The seeds had been planted, but it would be years before a personal tragedy made them take root. In the meantime, Kathy wanted to grow up to be a surgeon like her father. And so, it was presumed, did brother Tom.

Nine-year-old Kate (alias "Jimmy") at Fenwick. *The Homer Dickens Collection.*

Kate's brother Tom (second row, fourth from left) at the Kingswood Oxford School, 1917. *The Kingswood Oxford School.*

Family photo, 1920. Kate (far left) is 12. *The Ben Carbonetto Collection.*

Kate at 10, with her two-year-old sister Marion. *The Homer Dickens Collection.*

DR. HEPBURN'S SON, 15, HANGS HIMSELF WHILE VISITING IN NEW YORK

From the front page of *The Hartford Courant*—April 4, 1921.

Dead Body, Swinging From Curtain, Found by Sister in Home of Aunt—Despondency Suspected.

YOUTH ATHLETE AT KINGSWOOD SCHOOL

KINGSWOOD SCHOOL BOY WHO TOOK HIS LIFE IN NEW YORK

THOMAS N. HEPBURN, JR.

(Special to The Courant.)

New York, April 3.

Acting, it is believed, during a moment of morbid depression, Thomas N. Hepburn, jr., 15-years-old son of Dr. and Mrs. Thomas N. Hepburn of No. 352 Laurel street, Hartford, committed suicide by hanging some time Saturday night at the home of his adopted aunt, Mrs. Mary Towl of No. 26 Charlton street, Manhattan. The body was discovered yesterday morning by the boy's younger sister, Catherine, who went to his room to call him. As she entered the room, which is on an upper floor, she brushed against something, and, quickly recognizing the body of her brother, screamed for help. Mrs. Towl rushed to the room and it was found that the boy's body was suspended to a rafter overhead, climbing first on a packing case. The weight of the body had stretched the improvised rope and the knees were drawn up, so that the feet barely touched the floor.

Medical Examiner's Theory.

The medical examiner declared the boy was of a nervous disposition and had at one time been a sufferer from St. Vitus' dance. The theory that he might have witnessed a motion picture which had affected his mind was floated. It was said that the boy had seen but one picture during the week and that was a funny one. His father, who arrived at the Towl home this afternoon with Mrs. Hepburn, could give no reason for the boy's act, other than the belief that he had acted in a moment of morbid depression. With his sister the boy had been visiting Mrs. Towl since last Tuesday, and they planned to return to Hartford today. His trunk was packed Saturday night and all other preparations to leave were made.

At the Towl house it was said that just before retiring Saturday night the boy played several selections on his banjo.

Parents Are Summoned.

Little information concerning the tragedy could be learned last night at the Hepburn home, at No. 352 Laurel street, beyond the fact that Dr. and Mrs. Hepburn received a telegram about 11 o'clock yesterday morning summoning them to New York. They left almost immediately. A relative of Dr. Hepburn, who is staying at the house in the absence of the family, said no information had been received as to the details of the death.

The dead youth was the oldest of six children and a student at the Kingswood School on Farmington avenue. He was described as a bright, healthy, active boy, good in his studies and on the athletic field, being a football and baseball player. He was a member of the York Club of the school and was on the staff of the school paper.

Accompanied by an aunt and his sister, Catherine, he left Tuesday for New York to spend the Easter holidays with friends of the family, and it was expected that brother and sister would return today. At the Hepburn home it was said that Thomas apparently had not a care in the world and was among the happiest of boys. He was a diligent student, but was lively and cheerful and at all times seemingly in the best of spirits. It is said that Dr. Hepburn planned that his son should enter Yale at the completion of his preparatory studies and later study for the medical profession at Johns Hopkins, Baltimore, of which Dr. Hepburn is a graduate.

Praises Dead Boy.

Policeman Keefe, who does patrol duty at Laurel street and Farmington avenue, said he was well acquainted with young Hepburn and spoke in the highest terms of him. "He was the finest boy you'd want to meet," said the policeman, "always genial, riding around in his father's car with a bunch of his chums or children of the neighborhood. We used to see him at this corner nearly every night and he was always bright and lively, with a smile and a word for everybody. We'll miss him."

The Hepburns' new house on Bloomfield Avenue, to which the family moved in 1921. Kate's favorite climbing tree is at left. *University of Hartford.*

Kit (at right) looks on as friend and birth-control crusader Margaret Sanger delivers a speech in Washington, D.C. *The Bettmann Archive.*

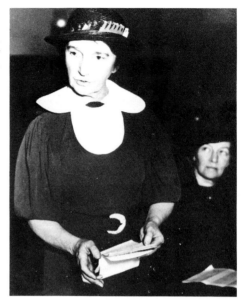

Sinclair Lewis in 1922, when he became Kate's new friend and confidante. *The Bettmann Archive.*

A 1922 photo of Kate, age 14, published in *The Hartford Daily Times* on August 18, 1923, upon her taking first place in a state golf tournament at Fenwick.

Kate in the 1928 Bryn Mawr
yearbook. *The Homer Dickens
Collection.*

Kate at 18. *The Homer Dickens
Collection.*

Kate (second from right, wearing blazer) in her first Bryn Mawr production, *The Truth About Blayds*, 1926. *The Homer Dickens Collection.*

Bob McKnight's bust of Kate at 21. *The Homer Dickens Collection.*

Kate as a barefoot Pandora in her senior year
at Bryn Mawr. *The Homer Dickens Collection.*

Kate at Fenwick, circa 1930.
The Homer Dickens Collection.

Kate and sisters Marion and Peggy, her remarkable looka-like, at the Hepburn family home, 1940. *Photo by Munkacsi, Courtesy Life Magazine.*

18.

I used to get up at dawn to do my homework because it was the only time the house was quiet enough to concentrate. But I hated to get up in the dark.

She had invited the British educator to Nook Farm to discuss the possibility of tutoring the sons of several prominent Hartford families, but Mrs. Bissell was not prepared for what arrived on her doorstep. George R. H. Nicholson stood 6 feet tall, weighed less than 150 pounds and, though it was the middle of summer, wore a raincoat *and* carried an umbrella. "I hadn't had a chance," Nicholson would recall, "to divest myself of my English customs."

It soon occurred to Nicholson that what the Bissells and their Nook Farm neighbors wanted was not a tutor so much as a school. What kind of a school, one of the Nook Farm parents asked suspiciously. "I don't know," Nicholson replied. "Just a damn good school." Sitting up that night in one of the guest rooms at the old Mark Twain house, Nicholson drew up a catalogue of courses that he later described as "like most catalogues, very vague, very optimistic and for all practical purposes, entirely worthless."

The Bissells were so taken with the idea that they moved out of the Mark Twain house and turned it over to Nicholson for his school for boys. He called it Kingswood after his alma mater, the Kingswood School in Bath.

Dr. Hepburn did not hesitate to sign up his eldest son. Filling out the blue admissions card, he declared that he intended for Tom to enter Harvard University. Under the heading "Hobbies or Particular Talents," Dr. Hepburn listed reading and stamp collecting. Sports: "Football, baseball, basketball, skating, swimming." No, Dr. Hepburn did not want his son to take music or dancing lessons at the school. To the question "Is he punctual and tidy?" Tom's father scrawled "Otherwise," then crossed it out and wrote "Yes." Dr. Hepburn added at the end that, while Kingswood would suffice for Tom's early teenage years, he intended to send him on to boarding school when he turned sixteen.

At 9 A.M. that first day of school, George R. H. (for "Raise Hell," his students speculated) Nicholson started out with nine pupils. The first order of business was to learn Kingswood's eight-point credo:

1. Accept a problem as a challenge just as kites rise against the wind.
2. Do one thing at a time and don't hurry.
3. Wear a cheerful face and walk with a vigorous carriage.
4. Work intensely on what is before you—then quit.
5. Look people directly in the eye. Think more of them than yourself.
6. Find an objective and go for it.
7. Develop a life apart from your work.
8. Don't think, act.

Tom flourished at Kingswood, earning high marks and eventually a letter in football. He was bright, athletic, popular, and as he grew into his middle teens, better-looking than Kathy—a handsome cross between his rugged father and the regal-looking Kit.

Much of Tom's success had to do with the unique environment at Kingswood, one of academic excellence tempered by humor and tolerance. Unlike more rigid headmasters, Nicholson was determined to let his students be boys. Mark Twain's glassed-in "Ombra" was a favorite spot for pitching pennies, and Nicholson liked nothing better than to burst out of his office door in mock indignation, sending Tom and the other boys scurrying.

On the last day of Tom's first year, one of the two staff teachers was out attending a wedding and another had fallen ill—leaving Nicholson alone to officiate at the long-planned track meet in which Tom was competing. "They had to have a starter, an announcer, a field judge, and one or two other officials," Nicholson later recalled. "So I remember quite distinctly standing at the beginning of a 100-yard dash firing the pistol and running to the other end of the track in order to judge the winners. Then I announced the score and the next events."

Tom continued to excel, joining Kingswood's "York" squad—which competed against the school's "Lancaster" squad in various athletic and academic contests—and the staff of the *Kingswood News*. In his fourth year, Tom was nominated for the student body's highest honor, Kingswood-Oxford's citizenship medal. Hep was so pleased with his eldest son's success that he wasted no time enrolling Kathy in Kingswood's sister institution, the Oxford School, in 1918. Over the next decade, all six Hepburn children would attend the Kingswood-Oxford Schools.

Oxford had been founded eight years earlier by a motherly, bespectacled schoolteacher named Mary Martin in two gray shingled houses on Oxford Street (from whence the school got its name). Kate later described the indomitable Miss Martin, who ran the school for twenty years, as "neat and sort of corseted and bosomed—she did her hair like mine now, *à la concierge*, and of course she was headmistress and represented power and respect. And that's what she got—respect."

Kathy's bike route—"Niles to Woodland to Asylum to Scarborough then left on Oxford"—changed when Oxford School moved to larger quarters at 510 Farmington Avenue in 1919. Now it was simpler—Laurel to Farmington, then a left and straight out.

Kathy's classroom was on the top floor of the three-story building. Miss Hunt taught history, Miss Stevenson algebra, Miss Ireland Latin, and Mlle Ricci taught French. A barn at the rear of the school had been turned into a combination gym and auditorium where a Mrs. Godfry taught "aesthetic dancing." Kathy thought it was *"antiseptic* dancing—I was a surgeon's daughter, you see."

Although Katharine Hepburn would in later years describe herself as not a particularly good student back at Oxford, her orange report card shows that her only weak subject, in the eighth grade, was Latin. She garnered top grades in History, Geography, Algebra, English, Art, French, and—astoundingly enough—Deportment.

If neither Latin nor "antiseptic" dancing captured her fancy, Kathy did continue her performing career, appearing in a charity benefit given by the Oxford school at the Hartford Club. The program for the evening shows "Catherine" Hepburn as one of the "Forget-Me-Nots" in "The Dance of the Flowers." She also began to show great promise as a figure skater and crack tennis player, though far and away her strongest sport was golf, which she played with an explosive temper. A classmate recalls the day they were playing together and Kathy missed a putt: "She threw her putter so that it stuck handle-down in the green and waved back and forth. *Poing!* We both laughed."

On the other hand, Kathy couldn't bring herself to laugh over her rivalry with Louise "Oisey" Taylor who, despite the billowing blue serge bloomers all Oxford girls were required to wear, always beat her in the high jump. ("That was irritating. She was tall. Oh, my dreams of floating over that bar. But no. She beat me. She just did.")

At twelve, Kathy also experienced her first schoolgirl crush—on Cathy Watson, her gym teacher. "Why Cathy, I don't know," Kate would remember. She had "a soft and gentle face, soft sandy hair—it was long and she did it in a knot and a velvet ribbon she wore around her head. I just remember that I thought about her and watched her and waited for her and brought her presents. I can't even remember what she sounded like—just love, it was. First crush." (Another classmate does not recall Cathy Watson in quite the same light: "She was a sturdy, squarish woman who seemed to have a permanent whistle in her mouth, which she blew right at me quite often.")

For now at least, Kathy found boys harder to appreciate. When she showed up at her first Kingswood-Oxford dance in a comfortably unstylish secondhand dress she had picked out herself, one of Tom's classmates gave him a nudge. "Who's that goofy-looking girl?" the boy laughed, just before Tom flattened him. "I was never going to be part of the club," recalls Kate. "But, being a Hepburn, I was used to that." (Even among Kathy's classmates, Mrs. Hepburn's battles against the "Antis" who opposed votes for women were well known. In a 1918 issue of the Oxford school journal, a poem by an anonymous student entitled "Just Imagine" included the following lines: "Just imagine / a class in which no one chews her pencil / no one whispering in study hall / Katharine Hepburn being an 'Anti' . . .")

That next summer at Fenwick, Tom won more races, and Kathy "ran along the beach, out to the lighthouse to see Mr. Knowles, the lighthouse keeper, shouting to myself as I ran how I was going to save the world. I think young girls have this powerful sense that, somehow, they're going to change the world."

Her mother already had. Kit had played a major role in winning the right for women to vote in Connecticut—a full year before ratification of the Nineteenth Amendment to the Constitution. Now she had a new, less weighty mission: At the age of forty-two, she was going to master the art of springboard diving. She installed a board at the end of the pier at Fenwick and, with Kathy hot on her heels, practiced jackknifes and flips. One sweltering day, Kit decided to dive without her long black stockings—standard bathing attire for the day. Kit's uncovered legs shocked Fenwickians that day far more than had her talk of prostitutes and venereal disease. She never dared bare all again.

On another afternoon, Kit turned around between dives to see her cousin Fannie Houghton Bulkeley. Fannie, a devout Anti, had been one of Kit's more strident critics. "Last year I voted for the first time," Fannie told Kit. "I liked it. I just want you to know that you were right and I was wrong." For this moment alone, Kit thought, it had all been worth it.

19.

I don't think they ever really knew what happened. It was a terrible blow.

The Hepburns were not a churchgoing lot, and that did not change merely because it was Easter Sunday. There was the traditional egg-coloring and egg hunt, followed by a typical Hepburn family feast attended by two dozen assorted uncles, aunts, cousins and in-laws. A hot topic of conversation among the adults: the controversial announcement by Kit's old friend and fellow suffrage campaigner Jo Bennett that she was giving away all her worldly possessions and trotting off with her husband to live in a log cabin in upstate Katonah, New York with a band of confirmed communists. Coinciding as it did with the arrest of the anarchists Sacco and Vanzetti, the Bennetts' declaration was, to say the least, unpopular among the solid citizens of Hartford at the Hepburns' that day.

Little of the adult talk could have meant anything to the Hepburn children, but Kit, very likely sensing their boredom, had a surprise for Tom and Kathy. She had never been particularly demonstrative toward the children—the occasional hug or pat on the head usually came from Dad, if it came at all. But Kit wanted Tom and Kathy, thirteen, to know how proud she was of their performance in school, and one way to do that was to reward them with a special vacation trip to see Aunty Mary Towle in New York two days hence.

A little after 2 P.M. the following Tuesday, March 29, 1921, Kit, Tom, and Kathy stepped off the train at Grand Central Station and hailed a cab for Greenwich Village. Mary Towle, taking a few days off from the law practice she shared with Bertha Rambaugh at 165 Broadway, was standing at the door of her four-story brick townhouse to greet them. They were each assigned rooms of their own—Kit's and Kathy's on the main floor, Tom's one flight up. For the next two days, the art-filled house at 26 Charleston Street served as home base for the free-spirited Aunty Towle and her spellbound guests.

The Hepburns soaked in the sights—Fifth Avenue, the museums, galleries, cafés, and shops—and even saw the famous Pavlova dance at the Metropolitan Opera House. But by the time Kit was ready to return home Thursday, Kathy and Tom wanted to see even more; they begged her to let them remain through the weekend. That afternoon, Kit waved goodbye to the kids as she climbed into a taxi that would take her back to Grand Central.

That Friday night, Kathy and Tom toured New York's fabled theater district for the first time. This was the Broadway of Ziegfeld and Cohan, and the names that lit up the marquees that night were among the greatest in the history of the stage: George Arliss in *The Green Goddess* at the Booth, Ruth Chatterton at the Empire playing *Mary Rose*, the legendary Mrs. Fiske in *Wake Up, Jonathan*, Laurette Taylor in *Peg O' My Heart* at the Cort, Jeanne Eagles in *In the Night Watch*, Ina Claire in *The Gold Diggers* . . .

What Kathy and Tom went to see at West 42nd Street's Selwyn Theatre was not live theater but, appropriately, a silent screen version of a story by Nook Farm's most famous resident. The advertisement in the *New York Times*, which managed to mispell in large type the name of the theater ("Selywn"), boasted that "for every LAUGH Mark Twain gave the world through the medium of his fanciful tale *A Connecticut Yankee in King Arthur's Court*, William Fox is affording two laughs with

Emmett J. Flynn's picturization of the book, with every Twain trick heightened, every laugh doubled, every smile broadened!" (Had she happened to glance at the *New York Times* theater listings that Friday morning, Kathy would have seen an article about the secret marriage of nineteen-year-old William Leland Hayward to Texas heiress Inez Gibbs, eighteen. A dozen years later, as show business agent Leland Hayward, he would fall deeply in love with his client Katharine Hepburn.)

The following day was spent at Central Park, and that evening Mary Towle invited a few young acquaintances over to meet Tom and Kath. Tom repaid this hospitality with an impromptu banjo recital, and several of the young ladies present teased him for being too handsome, too sensitive and arty. But Tom was accustomed, like all the Hepburn children, to being something of a "special" outsider. He took the mild chiding in stride, blushing just a little.

They had to catch a 10 A.M. train for Hartford the next day—Tom had purchased two tickets for parlor-car seats earlier that day—so shortly past ten that night Tom and Kathy retired to their rooms. Before starting upstairs, however, Tom took Aunty aside and thanked her for a wonderful time—"the most pleasant experience of my life."

Once in his room, Tom finished packing his things into a large suitcase. He changed into pajamas, then laid his trousers out neatly on a bureau, placing his suitcase on top of them so they'd stay freshly "pressed" for the next day's journey. He climbed into bed and turned off the light.

171

The next morning, Kathy and Aunty Towle waited until 8 A.M. for Tom to appear at the breakfast table. It had been an exhausting weekend, they reasoned—perhaps he had overslept. Finally Kathy went to wake him. She stood at the base of the stairs calling "Tom," then bounded up the steps, past an open bathroom door just off the landing, and down the hall toward his room.

She knocked on the door and called her brother's name again. Not a sound. She turned the doorknob and slowly pushed the door open. The first thing she saw were the trousers, neatly stretched out atop the dresser. The double bed had been slept in; one side of the covers had been disturbed. But still no sign of Tom. She moved into the room slowly, deliberately, then shuddered as her shoulder brushed against something hanging in the dark angle of a closet and wall. Kathy gasped for breath as she looked up to see Tom's stiff body, suspended from the rafters by a blue curtain tie. The weight of the body had stretched the makeshift hangman's rope taut. Tom's knees were buckled slightly, and his toes rested on the hardwood floor. Behind him was an overturned suitcase.

Kathy's screams for help brought Mary Towle in an instant, and they fumbled to untie the noose. They couldn't; it was knotted too tightly. While Aunty Towle rushed off to summon an ambulance, Kathy grabbed her brother's stiff body below the waist and held him up clear of the floor. That was how Dr. Condy of St. Vincent's Hospital found them when he arrived seventeen minutes later. The sight of Kathy, tears streaming down her face as she held up her brother, would stay with Dr. Condy for years. (An apocryphal account that appeared in the press has Kathy cutting her brother's body down, rushing to the doctor's house next door, and pleading with the maid who answered the door. "Please help," Kathy allegedly said, "my brother's dead." The maid then supposedly shrugged, "If he's dead, then the doctor can't help him," and slammed the door in her face.)

According to Dr. Condy, Tom could have died any time between midnight and 7 A.M. But judging from the condition of the body, the boy had probably been dead around five hours. That meant he would have gotten out of bed around 3 A.M. to fashion the hangman's noose and place it about his neck.

At 11 A.M., there was a knock on the door at 352 Laurel Street in Hartford. Kit Hepburn was not particularly concerned when she saw it was a uniformed Western Union agent; as a social crusader, she was more than accustomed to receiving wires. She opened the telegram and read the single sentence that would shatter her life.

The telegram from Mary Towle contained few details—only that Tom had been found dead. Dr. Hepburn at first refused to believe that his son might have committed suicide. How could the authorities explain the fact that Tom's feet were touching the floor? The boy may have been murdered, Dr. Hepburn told police over the telephone, and a clumsy effort made to disguise the crime. But then Tom's father had to abandon the desperate theory when it was explained to him that there had been no signs of an intruder entering the Towle house, nor had any unusual noises been heard coming from the victim's room during the night.

Dr. and Mrs. Hepburn boarded the noon train for New

York that day. Kit sat in stunned silence, staring blankly out the window at the still-barren countryside. What was happening seemed impossible. Her father, Alfred Houghton, had taken his life in a fit of melancholia, and now her eldest son had hanged himself for no apparent reason. She was of too rational a mind to believe that Tom had been the victim of some family curse or an inherited mental disorder that struck Houghton males. Yet the tragic coincidence seemed almost too much to bear.

When they arrived at Grand Central Station late that afternoon, Tom's grieving parents were met by a dozen shouting members of the press. How could Dr. Hepburn explain the tragedy? "God only knows why. My son was normal in mind and body, and the taking of his own life can be accounted for only from a medical point, that he was suddenly afflicted with adolescent insanity," he told reporters. "He was an athlete, bronzed with health and exercise. He won his colors with the football team of his school last fall, and had expressed his ambition to finish his studies at the preparatory school and enter Yale University, to study surgery, and as he said, 'follow in father's footsteps.' "

Monday morning, Dr. Hepburn returned to Connecticut and the hospital, where he could lose himself in his work. Kathy and Kit remained in New York, waiting to reclaim Tom's body from the medical examiner and accompany it to Hartford for burial.

Dr. Hepburn arrived home in time to see the *Hartford Courant* on the city's newsstands, blaring the news of Tom's death on its front page:

DR. HEPBURN'S SON, 15, HANGS HIMSELF WHILE VISITING IN NEW YORK

---

*Dead Body, Swinging From
Curtain, Found by Sister
in Home of Aunt—Despondency Suspected*

Youth Athlete at Kingswood School

Beneath a caption reading KINGSWOOD SCHOOL BOY WHO TOOK HIS LIFE IN NEW YORK, the *Courant* ran a recent school photo of Tom, a good-looking, tousle-haired young man in a school sweater. The expression on his face is both benign and haunting.

"The medical examiner declared the boy was of a nervous disposition and had at one time been a sufferer of St. Vitus's Dance," the *Courant* reported. "His father, who arrived at the Towle home this afternoon with Mrs. Hepburn, could give no reason for the boy's act, other than the belief he had acted in a moment of morbid depression." (The *Courant* story said Tom's body had been discovered by his sister "Catherine"; the *New York Times* identified her as "Clara.")

The portrait the *Courant* painted was one of a boy who had no earthly reason to end his life. "He was described as a bright, healthy, active boy, good in his studies and on the athletic field," the front-page story continued. "It was said that Thomas apparently had not a care in

---

the world and was among the happiest of boys. He was a diligent student, but was lively and cheerful and at all times seemingly in the best of spirits."

The piece ended by quoting Nook Farm's Officer Keefe. "He was the finest boy you would want to meet, always genial, riding around in his father's car with a bunch of his chums or children of the neighborhood," the policeman recalled. "We used to see him at this corner nearly every night and he was always bright and lively, with a smile and a word for everybody. We'll miss him."

The *New York Times* took the same why-did-he-do-it tack. The newspaper's page-six story was headlined:

MYSTERY IN SUICIDE
OF SURGEON'S SON

HARTFORD SCHOOLBOY, 15, VISITING
HERE, IS FOUND HANGING
IN HIS ROOM

WAS ATHLETIC AND HAPPY

*Must Have Killed Himself as Result of Suddenly
Developed Insanity, Father Says.*

"It was explained," noted the *Times* in the body of the piece, "that the boy was a normal, happy schoolboy, athletic and ambitious, though somewhat nervous in temperament. He had written cheerful letters to his parents, who were certain there was no sweetheart or

---

thwarted vocation or ambition involved, but that the tragedy must have been born of some sudden, irresistible impulse."

But there *was* a logical explanation, thirteen-year-old Kathy insisted. She phoned Daddy and asked him to remember the story he had told them about his undergraduate days back at Randolph-Macon, when to shock a visiting northern football team Hep and his buddies staged a mock lynching. The star of that particular show was a black who could tense his neck muscles so that he couldn't be choked. Tom had tried this stunt when he was fourteen, but stopped after he was warned of the danger. The same prank, however, was featured in *A Connecticut Yankee in King Arthur's Court*, the film version of which they had seen only the day before. Yes, her father allowed, Tom might have been tempted to try it again.

"I am convinced that I have done the boy an injustice," Dr. Hepburn said in a new statement to the *New York Times*. "In the first place, his whole life and temperament does not coincide with the suicide theory. While subject as a small boy to a few facial habits, he had outgrown them and was in the best mental condition that I have ever seen him. That he had no intention of taking his life is borne out by the fact that he had purchased tickets and parlor car seats for his return to Hartford with his sister . . . The bed showed that he had slept without restlessness, for it was only depressed in the spot where he lay. He left no note or sign of mental distress. To theorize that a normal, healthy boy committed suicide after a good night's sleep is unbelievable.

"I am now convinced that the boy was the victim of

an accident as the result of a foolish stunt. I had entirely forgotten that he considered himself an expert in hanging by the neck in such a way as to look as if he were dying, to the entertainment of his brothers and sisters. He used to fix a bowknot in the rope and untie it in time to prevent being choked. I warned him about a year ago of the danger of this stunt, but had not thought of it since that time.

"Friday night he saw a moving picture in which I am told there is . . . a hanging. That must have recalled his old stunt, and when he arose next morning he decided to rehearse it for a performance when he got home. He could find only a strip of cotton cloth to use, and the material was such that his bowknot did not slip as he expected. And so the poor boy was strangled to death as the result of a boyish idea.

"This accident theory would explain all the findings . . . In view of the fact that I have given the world my opinion, that the boy committed suicide, and have thereby cast a blot upon his memory, I feel anxious to repair this damage insofar as I am able."

Yes, yes it must have been a tragic accident—all the Hepburns wanted to believe this. They had to.

Accident or suicide, it hardly mattered as the reality of what had happened began to sink in. Tom's death at the age of fifteen was a crushing blow that would forever alter the dynamics of the Hepburn family, and Kathy's perception of the world.

20.

Naturally my brother's death flattened me emotionally. It was a major tragedy. Did it push me further into make-believe? Who knows? I would think it must have. It must have . . .

"I suppose it made me a more moody, suspicious person for a time," Kate was to recall. "But if I felt bad, you can imagine how my parents must have felt. They were devastated." Tom's death, says Kate, "threw me even closer to Dad and Mother. When we would speak together, it was a very different conversation than they would have had with anyone else. Our relationship was very, very close because they *made* it close. So did I."

Suddenly Kathy found herself cast in the role of eldest child. "It was as if, when Tom died, I sort of became two people instead of one—a boy and a girl," she explains. "That's why I practically raised the other kids. I was a third parent—my younger brothers and sisters were more like my own children than my brothers and sisters."

Within the family, Kathy eagerly embraced her new role and the added responsibilities it entailed. "Oldest daughters are often called upon to do this," Kate observes. "That's why there are so many oldest daughters who don't marry. By the time they've grown up, they feel as if they've already raised a family."

Kathy's attitude to the outside world changed. As she admits, she became increasingly moody, suspicious, even hostile—traits that would eventually help shape her image as one of Hollywood's most temperamental stars.

For a thirteen-year-old, however, such fundamentally antisocial behavior was cause for concern. Two months after her return to school, Kathy's grades slipped so markedly—she was now flunking Latin altogether—that her parents pulled her out of Oxford and hired a tutor.

William O. Williams was, in fact, on the staff of

Kingswood-Oxford. The mahogany plaque honoring his memory at the school's Seaverns Hall reads *Omnes omnia docebat*—"He taught everybody everything." "Wow," as he came to be known, was Kingswood-Oxford's faculty troubleshooter, hired out to tutor male and female students in need of an academic boost. A small, soft-spoken Englishman, he was just as eccentric a soul as any of the Hepburns. Wow listened to Handel for hours on his Victrola, brewed tea over a Bunsen burner, and when he could get away with it, defiantly drove his Packard on the left-hand side of the road.

What won Kathy and his other students over was not so much Wow's Mr. Chips facade (after twenty years in the U.S., he still persisted in calling a washcloth a "face flannel"), as his mesmerizing accounts of his own adventures. He had at various times driven his motorcycle across Europe, hunted bobcats in Vermont, and fought off bandits in Egypt.

Yet another, even more nimble storyteller arrived at the Hepburns' new house on West Hartford's Bloomfield Avenue late that summer. He was gangly and stooped, with a wispy thatch of orange hair, a receding chin, and a red face pitted with acne scars. He had, much to his misfortune, inherited his mother's looks. His name was Sinclair Lewis.

Like Kathy, Lewis was the child of a doctor and, while growing up in Sauk Centre, Minnesota, came to consider himself something of a misanthrope. Also like Kathy, his nickname was "Red." At ten, he had almost drowned. Then, three years later, the Sauk Centre *Herald* reported that young Lewis had run away to sign up as a drummer boy with U.S. forces fighting in the Spanish-

181

American War—only to be dragged back home by his angry father. He was greeted by a group of delinquents singing "Yankee Doodle Dandy," and for the next several years was derisively called "Doodle."

"I am seventeen," Lewis scrawled in his diary on January 1, 1903. "Tall, ugly, thin, red-haired but not, methinks, especially stupid. I am in the academy of Oberlin College." From there he went to Yale, then on to a career as a journalist, editor, and hack writer—until his breakthrough in 1920 with the unexpected critical and commercial success of his biting, satirical novel on life in a small midwestern town, *Main Street.*

Less than two years later, Red Lewis was heading for Connecticut. While awaiting the publication of his next book, *Babbitt,* Lewis, like Twain before him, was lured by the literary tradition of Hartford. In the fall of 1921, Lewis and his wife Grace moved into a prepossessing house at 25 Belknap Road. Built to the specifications of a wealthy woman who had spent a substantial portion of her youth in Florence, the Lewises' new residence boasted a gracefully curved stairway with a marble fountain at its base, a mahogany-paneled library, a minstrel gallery, and a guest room with an elaborately carved canopy bed *and* a shrine.

Two weeks later, the author was grousing to his friend H. L. Mencken that "we seem to have settled in this town which has no virtues except that one can live in a lordly manner on not very much money, and that though it's quiet for work, it's also only three hours from NY. I have never yet been able to find where in these beatific *Vereinigen* I could be content to live more than a few months. This is another experiment: we have leased a house for a year." For her part, Grace hosted a series of Sunday morning breakfasts that proved a bona fide hit with the local crowd of aspiring young writers.

Angered that the Hartford establishment all but ignored the city's great literary tradition while glorying in its commerce (ironically, the author could not have known that in the nearby offices of the Hartford Accident and Indemnity Company a young insurance executive named Wallace Stevens was working on his first volume of poetry), Lewis managed within a few weeks of arriving to offend nearly every important hostess in town—a feat that impressed even the outcast Hepburns.

What sped up the process, predictably, was alcohol. After a few drinks, Lewis was all too likely to start swearing. When one hostess objected, he stormed out of the house in a rage. Or he might simply rise from the table at a dinner party, declare he was tired, and seek out the nearest available bed.

The most celebrated incident was recounted in the *Bridgeport Herald:*

> Then came the party at the home of Mr. and Mrs. C. Morgan Aldrich, where the pink of Hartford's younger set gathered, including the Lewises. The party became somewhat gay, and Lewis, who is an irreverent fellow, as everybody knows, got to singing a song which has been sung by college fellows more times than a few. The song contained one or two irreligious passages, not obscene but making

fun of sacred things. The song was objectionable to Mrs. Aldrich, so the story goes, and
Lewis was requested to stop singing it. Lewis,
seeing nothing objectionable in his song, was
displeased and insisted on singing it or quit-
ting the party. The host and hostess are said
to have stood by their original contention that
the song was too irreverent to be sung in their
home, and the Lewises left the house . . . The
Aldriches had decreed "thumbs down" on the
Lewises and Lewis had become dissillusioned
about Hartford.

Yet early in his Hartford period, Lewis did hit upon
a new idea for a book about the medical profession. He
began reading up on bacteriology and talking to the
knowledgeable likes of Hartford Hospital's own O. C.
Smith.

At one affair hosted by the Bissells, Lewis was, as
usual, succumbing to crashing boredom until he was at
long last introduced to a person with something to say:
Kit Hepburn. His fascination with her was twofold—
she was clearly the single most interesting woman he
had met in Hartford, and her husband could be a valuable source of information for his new book.

"He met Mother again at another party," recalls Kate,
"and he said to her 'Why haven't you called me?' You
see, he was gathering information for *Arrowsmith*, and
I think he wanted to know Dad.

"Mother said, 'You go home now and I'll call for you.'
And then she invited them [Red and Gracie Lewis] to

dinner. And she knew that Lewis drank a fair amount, and Daddy would not purchase alcohol. He would drink if it was given to him, but he would not purchase it.

"So Mother said, 'We can't have Mr. Lewis to dinner unless we have some whiskey and soda,' so Daddy said 'Why not?' Daddy called him up and said 'Listen, if you have to get drunk to stand me, you better bring your own, because we don't serve it.' And he never drank when he came to the house." (Dr. Hepburn's own philosophy regarding the consumption of alcohol was simple: "Drink only when you're happy, never to escape. You can't face a problem if you're too drunk to recognize it.")

Soon Red Lewis found himself drawn to the brooding young girl with flashing eyes, red hair like his, and the most unusual voice he had ever heard. They both had an insatiable sweet tooth, and Kathy would share one of her favorite goodies with Lewis—a "poisonous concoction" of marshmallow and chocolate atop a vanilla cookie that she picked up regularly at Murphy's grocery store. ("So fine for the teeth and digestion that they stopped making it.")

"I remember going on Sunday walks with Red Lewis," says Kate. "We used to shinny up little trees, little willow trees that were very bendable, little birch trees, and he couldn't shinny, but he could look up at me in wonder.

"I can remember we were supposed to kiss him good-bye on Sundays. He had the most terrible . . . he was redheaded, and his skin is like mine—*destroyed* by the sun. Anyway, he'd kneel down so we could kiss him and I'd think, 'Oh, God.' But I'd do it, of course.

"He was great fun, a nice man, and Gracie Lewis was a very glamorous dresser . . . They were just sort of part of our lives."

Lewis also became a regular guest at Fenwick, dropping off his son Wells (named after his great friend H. G. Wells) to spend the summer months in the company of children his own age—namely the Hepburn and Hooker broods.

Meantime, the author's primary professional objective at Hartford had been achieved. Hep had provided Lewis with whatever insights he could into the inner workings of the medical profession. The result, *Arrowsmith*, would earn Lewis a 1926 Pulitzer Prize. Still stung by the Pulitzer jury's refusal to give the award to either *Main Street* or his masterpiece *Babbitt*, he refused to accept the prize for *Arrowsmith*. (Lewis went on to become the first American awarded the Nobel Prize for Literature, in 1930, for a body of work that also included *Elmer Gantry* and *Dodsworth*. After divorcing Gracie, Lewis was married to the celebrated journalist Dorothy Thompson from 1928 until their own divorce in 1942. By way of another ironic coincidence, Thompson was proclaimed "Woman of the Year" in 1935 by the popular novelist Mary Roberts Rinehart. Rinehart's son married a Houghton cousin of Kate Hepburn's, and in 1942 Kate portrayed a character based on Thompson in her first movie with Spencer Tracy, *Woman of the Year*.)

Red Lewis was among only a handful of close friends in whom Kathy confided to help her through the difficult and confusing years after Tom's death. But her real escape came, as it did for millions of others, sitting in a darkened theater and dreaming she was someone else.

"Silent pictures fascinated me from the very first," Kate recalls. Most often she went with her father to the Empire Theater, which specialized in "westerns and action—William S. Hart, Tom Mix, that style of movie. Dad loved the horses."

Kathy shared Heps' passion for shoot-'em-ups— "William S. Hart was my particular favorite"—but whenever she got the chance she would sneak away to the Majestic Theater, where "the more romantic stuff" was playing. Since no Hepburn child ever received an allowance per se, Kathy shoveled walks and raked leaves to earn the money for admission. Mary Ryan, the seamstress who had so patiently sat through Kathy's amateur theatrics, was now privy to another terrible secret: with the few nickels she had left over, Kathy was splurging on movie magazines. In blissful solitude at the Majestic, Kathy whiled away whole afternoons gazing up at the flickering, larger-than-life images of Mary Pickford ("Everyone loved her. I was no exception"), Gloria Swanson, Rudolph Valentino, Lillian Gish, Ramon Navarro, and an intriguing newcomer named Greta Garbo. "My favorite movie actress by far was Leatrice Joy," says Kate. "She was married to John Gilbert at the time, and I thought she was absolutely sensational. One of her best pictures, I think, was *A Man's Lawyer*, with Thomas Mann playing a cop to her rich lady. At an early age, I found that captivating."

Kathy dreamed of becoming one of them. "Oh, yes," she concedes, "I saw myself as someday becoming a movie star. It seemed perfectly natural for me, and from the very minute I did my first screen test years later, I thought it was a very easy medium because if you didn't get it right the first time, you could do it again. Besides, I always thought theater audiences were out to get me."

The adolescent girl watching Valentino smolder in *The Sheik* knew nothing of this, of course. For her, the one word that best described the moviegoing experience would become a mainstay of her vocabulary: "Thrilling."

21.

Mother was always telling us
kids that they'd planned to have
us, that we weren't mistakes. I
was glad to hear it.

The question was whether Kit Hepburn and Margaret Sanger had everything or nothing in common. Both had lived in Corning at about the same time, yet they never met. Sanger (Maggie Higgins then), five years younger than Kit and the violet-eyed daughter of a hard-drinking Irish tombstone-carver, was content to admire the elegant Houghton girls from her vantage point on the wrong side of the tracks. Both had mothers who died young of cancer. Both were beautiful, educated, red-haired, give-'em-hell left-wing firebrands. Both were still quite young when they married handsome, dynamic, successful professional men, though Kit would stick with hers and Margaret wound up divorcing, then taking on numerous lovers (including free-love proponent Havelock Ellis and H. G. Wells) before marrying a second time.

So Kit's mother was one of those grand parasol-twirling ladies Margaret had envied from afar, and with good reason. Margaret's memories were of growing up cold and hungry with ten brothers and sisters (survivors of her mother's eighteen pregnancies). The Higginses were so poor that when Margaret's four-year-old little brother died, her mother had no photo to remember him by. So Margaret's father sneaked into the cemetery around midnight, dug up the boy's coffin and, with ten-year-old Margaret holding the lantern, made a plaster cast of the boy's face. From the death mask, he fashioned a bust for his grief-stricken wife.

Her first job as a public health nurse confirmed what Margaret had learned from painful personal experience: that among poor families in particular, birth control was essential. Even before she focused on contraception as an issue, Margaret hobnobbed with the radical activists of the day, including "Big Bill" Haywood, the one-eyed giant of a labor leader (he had lost an eye in a mine explosion), Clarence Darrow, and muckraker Lincoln Steffens. She also became a compatriot (and later arch-rival) of Kit's friend Emma Goldman. In addition to a passionate commitment to socialism, Sanger and Goldman shared Havelock Ellis's desire to bring about a sexual revolution—one that would liberate men and women from the "fraud" of monogamy.

In 1915 Margaret Sanger almost singlehandedly launched the family-planning movement in the United States . . . and was promptly indicted for distributing birth-control information through the mails. Her new friend John Reed, who would later write the monumental *Ten Days That Shook the World*, rushed to Margaret's defense. First he suggested that she reverse the public perception of her as a screaming radical by hiring Underwood and Underwood (Kit's favorite photographers) to take a portrait of her in a black dress with a starched Quaker collar, her two young sons standing beside her. Newspapers across the country printed the photograph, transforming her image overnight.

Next, Reed hosted a dinner in Margaret's honor at New York's Brevoort Hotel the night before her trial. Walter Lippmann was there to lend support, and so, much to Margaret's surprise and delight, was Kit Hepburn.

Kit listened as Margaret began by flattering her audience. "I know that all of you are better able to cope with the subject than I am," she allowed. "I know that physicians and scientists have a fund of information

greater than I have on the subject of family limitation
. . . There is nothing new, nothing radical in birth control. Aristotle advocated it; Plato advocated it; all our
great modern thinkers have advocated it.

"Yet all this scientific and technical discussion has only
had the effect of producing more technical and scientific
discussion—all very necessary and very stimulating to
that very small group of men and women who could
understand it. But all during the long years this matter
has been discussed, advocated, refuted, the people
themselves—the poor people especially—were blindly,
desperately practicing family limitation—just as they are
practicing it today. To them birth control does not mean
what it does to us. To them it has meant the killing of
babies, infanticide, abortions. Women from time im-
memorial have tried to avoid unwanted motherhood.
We all know the tribe of professional abortionists which
have sprung up and profited by this terrible misfortune.

"We know, too, that when the practice of abortion
was put under the ban by the church, an alternate evil—
the foundling asylum, with its horrifying history—
sprang up. There is no need to go into the terrible facts
concerning the recklessness, the misery, the filth, with
which children have been and still are being brought
into the world.

"I merely want to point out the situation I found when
I entered the battle. On the one hand, I found wise men,
sages and scientists, discussing birth control among
themselves. But their ideas were sterile. They did not
influence or affect the tremendous facts of life among
the working classes and the disinherited.

"How could I bridge this chasm? How could I reach these people? How could I awaken public opinion to this tremendous problem?

"I might have taken up a policy of safety, sanity, and conservatism, but would I have got a hearing?

"And as I became more conscious of the vital importance of this idea, I felt myself in the position of one who has discovered that a house is on fire, and I found that it was up to me to shout out the warning! The tone of the voice may have been indelicate and unladylike, and was not at all the tone that many would rather hear.

"But this very gathering—this honor you have thrust upon me—is ample proof that intelligent and constructive thought has been aroused. Some of us may only be fit to dramatize a situation—to focus attention upon obsolete laws, like this one I must face tomorrow morning. Then, others, more experienced in constructive organization, can gather together all this sympathy and interest which has been aroused, and direct it.

"I thank you for your encouragement and support. My request to you tonight is that all you social workers— so much better fitted to carry on this work than I—that you consider and organize this interest. This is the most important step, and only in this way can I be vindicated! Let us put the United States of America upon the map of the civilized world!"

Margaret's speech brought her audience to its feet and caused such a national furor that the authorities dropped the charges against her. (The following year, however, she would be arrested and thrown in jail for starting a birth-control clinic in Brooklyn.)

Kit believed devoutly in what Sanger was trying to do, but for Kathy's embattled mother it was a question of priorities. Suffrage had always had first claim on her energies, followed by the twin dilemmas of prostitution and venereal disease. It was precisely because Margaret Sanger seemed to have matters so well in hand that Kit felt that she could postpone her own involvement.

But then, seven years later—the year after Tom's death—Kit was ready for a new cause, ready to lose herself in a new crusade. At a time of life when women were expected to settle gracefully into complacent middle age, forty-four-year-old Kit yearned for new heights to conquer. "When you decide to climb to the top of the mountain," she liked to tell Kathy, "there is no reason to stop midway because you are tired. The world is dominated by power, and you'd better not be weak if you can help it." The fight for a more enlightened attitude toward birth control seemed a logical next step for Kit. "After the suffrage fight," she later recalled, "I got into birth control because I felt that women would always be hopelessly handicapped if they did not have control of how many children they produced. Suffrage woke them up a little. I felt that if they were awakened to what they could do in this world, only then would they be fully developed human beings. Anything that helps women develop their own inherent capacity is good for them and good for the world. Besides, what good is the vote if women don't have power over their own bodies?"

With her own children she had always been unswervingly candid on the subject of sex. "If you aren't frank with your children about sex," she told a stunned New

Haven Methodist Church group, "they will never con-
fide in you again." When Kit "scientifically and specifically" described the procreative act for Kathy, the young
girl replied "Oh, then I can have a baby without getting
married. Then that's what I'll do—unless perhaps I can
find a husband as nice as Dad."

Once again, the entire Hepburn tribe was recruited to
march in picket lines, lick envelopes, and hand out
pamphlets. For her part, Kit saw absolutely nothing in-
consistent about a mother of six waving the banner for
contraception. "I believe all women want children," she
conceded to a Hartford newspaper reporter. "It is a
maternal instinct. But they also want to take care of
their children properly and educate them. It is agony
of the first order when they can't do these necessary
things."

If anything, Kit became even more passionate about
the contraception issue than she had been about her
other causes. "Women need birth control even more
than they needed the vote," she reasoned, because while
some conservative women as well as men were opposed
to suffrage, "almost every woman believes in birth control. Birth control is an obvious necessity to the average
woman." Ultimately, she concluded, "a woman ought
to have some say in the number of children she has. I
believe in the freedom for men and women to determine
the size of their family. Why should they have fifteen
children if they can take care of only two?"

While in 1922 it remained a crime throughout the
country to distribute birth-control information, the
Hepburns' beloved Connecticut remained the only state
in the union where it was still a crime to *use* contracep-

tion. (That law, though obviously unenforceable, remained on the books into the 1980s, upheld by Federal Judge [and controversial Supreme Court nominee] Robert Bork.)

Kit led the attack on home turf as founder and first president of the Connecticut Birth Control League—eventually to become Planned Parenthood. Once again she made stirring speeches at Carnegie Hall, traveled about the country (in 1922 alone Kit took the birth control message to Massachusetts, New York, Oklahoma, Illinois, and Pennsylvania), and haunted the corridors of power in Washington. She had become accustomed to indifference and hostility, but she was appalled at the childish manner in which even the most powerful politicians chose to react to what she had long regarded as a fundamental human-rights issue. Like nearly everyone else in straightlaced society, most of these men were incapable of discussing condoms, douches, and diaphragms with a straight face. When Kit first took her case for a liberalized birth-control bill to Congress, committee members behaved like "dirty-minded little boys. They poked one another, giggled and put their hands before their faces."

At the heart of her commitment to the birth-control movement was Kit's deep affection for Margaret Sanger. "She is a great friend," Kit would often say, "and I admire her tremendously. She is not strong, but she has the devotion of a saint to the cause." Yet there remained strong differences of opinion between the two advocates, particularly on the issues of marriage and fidelity. Kit saw contraception strictly as a way of lessening the eco-

nomic burden on married couples. Sanger also saw it
as a way to make women as sexually liberated as men.

In her role as Sanger's chief strategist and federal legislative chairman, Kit was all business on the Hill. Kit
Hepburn had, Sanger later recalled, "learned great ef-
ficiency and was so careful of minutiae that she never
let our witnesses run over their time." If a congressman
speaking on behalf of liberalizing birth-control laws
looked as if he was losing his audience, Kit would slip
him a note warning "Time up in one minute!" Before
one particularly loquacious senator rose to speak, Kit
held onto his coattail and said "I'll give you a signal
when it's time to stop." She did, but he kept on talking.
Again, she gave his coattail a yank, firmer this time. The
man droned on. Finally, she reached over—with both
hands this time—and pulled him, still sputtering, down
into his seat.

During one debate, Kit listened calmly as a zealous
young priest argued the church line that contraception
ran counter to God's natural order. Then, when it was
her turn to speak, she asked the father why he was
wearing a pair of eyeglasses. Was it not God's will that
he endure blurred vision? And how could he remain
celibate when clearly "nature's way" was to propagate
the species? The priest, his face now a bright crimson,
smiled wanly as laughter filled the auditorium. Kit
chalked up another victory. But it had only been a skir-
mish. She would not live to see the Pill bring about an
end to the war.

(Kate herself, in the late 1970s and the 1980s, picked
up the pro-choice banner, writing letters for Planned

Parenthood that raised millions of dollars in contributions for that organization's fight against a proposed constitutional amendment outlawing abortions. "Dear Friend," began her first letter, "Normally, I don't get involved in public controversy. But reproductive freedom is a basic, *personal* issue, and one that I feel very strongly about for personal reasons. Over fifty years ago, my mother helped Margaret Sanger found a new, controversial organization . . . that later became Planned Parenthood, and since then has been in the forefront of providing family planning services to millions of Americans. Now I have joined Planned Parenthood in carrying on my mother's struggle so many years later because proposed legislation could destroy all of her tireless work. So far," she continued, "the loudest voices have been those of the militant anti-abortionists who have screamed loudest with such hostile slogans as 'Stop the Baby Killers.' There are people who hold deep religious beliefs which forbid abortion. But they conduct their own lives according to their own beliefs and do not attempt to impose those beliefs on the rest of us. Those are not the people who pose a danger to individual rights. What deeply troubles me, however, is that a minority is using whatever political power they can muster to force their point of view on you and me. *The fight is far from over.*" In 1987, she was anything but sanguine about the situation. "It's so much worse now," she told me. "The right-to-lifers are trying to redefine what a human life *is*. I have yet to see a funeral for a miscarried fetus. Why must women be victims of their fertility?"

Kathy was intensely proud of her mother's achievements, but as a teenager it was Dad she chose to emulate. With Tom gone, the job of following in her father's sizable footsteps as a surgeon fell to Kathy. And, more than anything else, she wanted to please him.

She also sought to fill the void left by her brother on the playing field, by becoming a crack tennis player, a bronze-medal-winning figure skater, and an expert diver. Still, her strongest game was golf, and by her mid-teens Kathy showed signs of becoming one of the finest women golfers in the country. (Katharine Hepburn's athletic prowess would eventually inspire her friends Garson Kanin and Ruth Gordon to write *Pat and Mike*, the 1952 hit comedy about a professional sportswoman and her manager. In the film, one of nine starring Tracy and Hepburn, Tracy delivers the famous line about Kate: "Not much meat on her, but what's there is cherce.") In August of 1923, fifteen-year-old Kathy landed in the sports pages of the Hartford papers as winner of the annual woman's golf tournament in Fenwick. The following year she ranked second in the state among juniors.

Whatever the sport, Kathy was fiercely competitive. "When my best friend won a prize for a simple front dive and I didn't win a prize for my fancy Dutchman's dive, I nearly died of fury!"

Scene: Kathy is playing a friendly game of tennis with one of her cousins, and she does not notice at first that her father and one of the young doctors from the hospital have dropped by to watch. It seems an even enough match; Kathy is winning, but not by much. She's not really trying all that hard. When she catches her father and his colleague out of the corner of her eye, however, she turns into a hellion on the court, demolishing her opponent.

———————

"Dad always said 'You play rotten golf when you play with me, but if there is anyone standing on the tee, you're sensible enough not to miss it,' " she remembers. "What he was saying was true enough: Once I had an audience I *had* to win."

22.

Danger intoxicates me.

It had all started with the breakneck sled rides hanging on to the rear bumper of Dad's Maxwell, and with that trapeze suspended high above the gravel drive. Now in her teens, Kathy was looking for new thrills, new challenges—a little risky business. There were only so many games of prisoner's base one could play, only so many birches to be climbed. That was all well and good for her younger brothers and sisters. As for boys, at fifteen Kathy was still not quite ready just yet. There was enough "Jimmy" left in her to make even the thought "slightly nauseating."

Allie Barbour, who had played Beauty to Kathy's donkey-headed Beast at Fenwick, shared her friend's growing ennui. So when she cooked up The Plan, Kath was more than eager to tag along. When September rolled around, Fenwick's wealthy families closed up their massive summer "cottages" and headed back to Hartford with their youngsters to start another school year. Kath and Allie, however, had tutors, so they remained to embark on what Kate would later call her "life of crime."

With their occupants out of town, the empty homes were "too tempting to resist. We'd break into random houses," she confesses, "and I became a real expert on knowing whether a house was open or closed, whether anyone was in—spotting a window someone may have left unlocked . . ."

There were other avenues of entry: "In those days the iceman used to deliver ice through an outside door, and that door could be pried open. So I'd get in that way and then let my friend in." Other times, Kathy shinnied up a trellis or a drainpipe, climbed through an upstairs window, then sauntered casually downstairs to let her accomplice in through the front door. "I could get up on any roof—still can today," Hepburn claims. "Right up the gutter pipe, in, and nothing could ever keep me out. I could break in, look over a place, and get in and out faster than any teenager in juvenile court."

If it hadn't been for Allie's egging her on, Kate insists, she never would have had the courage to break-and-enter on her own. "Being naturally timid, I could never do it alone." Once Kath had fingered a joint as vulnerable, it was her friend who gave the orders. "She'd say, 'We're going in here,' and I'd say, 'Oh, do you think we ought to?' and she'd say, 'Yes, you go up and drop through the skylight.' I'd say, 'All right,' and I'd go through the skylight, throw a rope down to her and lug her up. I don't have too much nerve on my own—people think I do, but I don't. But I have a great ability when I get prodded."

Usually, Kathy and Allie just snooped around freely, taking satisfaction in knowing that they were breaking the law and getting away with it. Only once did such an escapade escalate to include burglary. "One house we broke into was called the Whitmarsh House, and after I let Allie in I came across a crocodile nutcracker. It fascinated me, so I stole it." Once she got it home, however, "I was so overcome with guilt that I broke back into the house and put the crocodile nutcracker back where it belonged. From then on, I'd be content with just casing the joint."

That didn't make Kathy's little avocation any less hazardous. "I was a real second-story woman, climbing through windows and skylights. Why I lived, I don't know. I did the most dangerous things." Her closest brush with the Almighty came when the two girls invaded the Newton Brainard house, summer home of Hartford's mayor.

Kathy somehow managed to climb up onto the roof of the house, where she intended to lower herself through an open skylight. Making her way along the rooftop in the dark, she lost her footing and pitched head-first through the opening. In that last split second, she managed to catch herself on the skylight frame, hanging by her fingers above the cold marble floor three stories below. She caught her breath and slowly pulled herself back up. More than sixty years later, she still shivers when she tells the story. *"Terrifying.* I damned near dropped the whole three stories. It was just by the grace of God that I didn't."

Even this hair-raising scare was not enough to stop them. It would take an outsider to ruin what until then had been Kathy's perfect criminal record. Allie Barbour asked if she could spice things up a bit by bringing along her new "admirer," a good-looking if somewhat brash preppy named Bob Post. Kath grudgingly agreed, and soon came to regret it.

That night's target was the gabled Victorian manse of the eminent Dr. Francis Goodrich. A challenge. At first glance, the Goodrich house more closely resembled an impenetrable fortress than a seaside vacation cottage, and on further inspection, Kath concluded, it was just that: impenetrable.

KATH: There is no way we can get it.

ALLIE: Are you sure, Kath?

KATH: Positive. After all, you can't just smash in the back door.

BOB: Sure you can.

KATH: Sure you can what?

BOB: Smash in the back door.

With that, Hepburn recalls, "He got a big log, and then he said, 'Now, hold onto it, girls, and we'll just ram it.' And we did. We rammed it and bashed in the back door."

That wasn't all. "We took talcum powder from the bedroom, and threw a great big feather muff all over. The stuff got into the cracks of the paneled walls, and it cost endless amounts of money to get it out of the wall."

As it turned out, "The cook next door was watching the whole thing. Everyone knew that we'd done it, so we hardly had to confess. Bob Post was, I think, a bad lot. I mean he was *Allie's* boyfriend, not mine."

The burden of making restitution was assumed by Dr. Hepburn. "Dad paid to fix the door and the walls," says Kate, "but he didn't really punish me. I think he understood the thrill, and that we were overcome with guilt. That was the last house we broke into, obviously. The end to my life of crime."

To atone, Kath decided to make at least a stab at polite society. At sixteen, she had blossomed into a full-blown dazzler. The flame-red mane, blue-gray eyes and high, chiseled cheekbones just beginning to emerge intrigued the Yalies and Harvard boys who came home to Hartford on weekends and holidays. She even joined the Hartford Junior Assembly, though the kinds of boys this affiliation attracted—safe, conservative, conventional—were not exactly her parents' cup of tea. Not that a Bolshevik spouting revolution would have met with a warmer reception; like all fathers of teenage girls, Dr. Hepburn took great pleasure in watching Kath's beaus squirm under his withering stare. He tended to dismiss the whole lot as "excruciatingly boring." Later he told his daughter, "I'd have to sit with those goddamn men and I'd have to talk to them, and I'd think, 'If she marries any of them, it's going to be hell.' "

If a potential suitor was lucky enough to drop by when Dr. Hepburn was in surgery, he still had to contend with Kit. She would politely offer the young man tea, and while she poured it for him would ask where he stood politically. When the best the boy could do was mimic his parents' Republican beliefs, Kit would invariably sigh, "How dull. How *awfully* dull," and politely but promptly usher him out, *sans* Kathy.

To be sure, a visit to the Hepburn home was not for the faint of heart. Even if a beau of Kath's passed muster with Kit and made it to the dinner table, he usually had to fend for himself despite the plethora of servants. Brothers, sisters, uncles, aunts, cousins, and assorted hangers-on would invariably be making their way in and out of the kitchen with platefuls of food. The only hard and fast rule here was that Dad carved the meat—a task for which he, as a surgeon, seemed indisputably qualified. A typical first course for any Hepburn family meal would be Kit baiting her unflappable husband on some political issue. That would be followed by a hefty helping of chaos as everyone—children included—jumped into the fray on one side or the other. Just as the outsider prepared to duck for cover, someone—often Kath—would make a remark that caused the rest of the clan to shriek with laughter.

At Fenwick years later, one young man managed to fit in so well that he might have been mistaken for a member of the family. He was a crack sailer and tennis player, an intelligent (and decidedly free-thinking) debater, and handsome to boot. After the boy thanked his generous hosts for a wonderful weekend and departed, Kit commented on Kath's nice young man. Yes, Kath agreed, but she hadn't invited him. And, no, he wasn't a classmate of either Dick's or Robert's. As it happened, no one had invited him. The fellow was nothing more than a charming gate-crasher.

In the summer of 1924, Kath was preparing for a bit of gate-crashing of her own. She still planned to become a surgeon like her father, to follow in Hep's footsteps the way Tom would have, had he lived. "You know, I can't answer how I got into acting," she concedes, still mystified at the course her life took. "I really wanted to be a doctor, that's all. There was no question that I was going to study medicine."

By enrolling in her mother's alma mater, Kath was also carrying on a cherished tradition among the Houghton women. "Actually," shrugs Kate, "I hadn't picked it. It was just one of those things—all the girls in our family went there, and so I had to go. Dad and Mother wanted me to have a degree, and, frankly, I couldn't think of anything better to do."

As her mother had done nearly thirty years before, Kath crammed with the help of a tutor to pass the Bryn Mawr entrance exams. "I was *brilliant* in biology. That made sense to me," she says. "But I was a real dunce in physics. Didn't have the vaguest idea what it was all about. After a summer's tutoring, I went from a 69 to a 71—just two points!" Nevertheless, that was all she needed to pass the entrance exams. "I didn't think I was necessarily dumb, but life was so . . . thrilling."

23.

I got in by the skin of my
teeth, and by the skin of my
teeth I stayed.

The young woman who got off the train at Bryn Mawr station that September was "completely unprepared" for the scholastic rigors of college life. Things had changed considerably in the quarter-century since Kit had graduated. The "lantern man" who met students at the train station and escorted them to the campus at night was no longer there; by 1924, Bryn Mawr girls could be expected to watch out for themselves. M. Carey Thomas was also gone, replaced by Marion Edwards Park. President Park, who was such a lover of classical music that every commencement at which she presided was accompanied by a chamber orchestra, had an able assistant in Dean Helen Taft Manning. Dean Manning's father was William Howard Taft.

Any girl living away from home for the first time might expect to feel homesick, but for Kathy the gnawing anxiety was tenfold. Her family had been her world; tutored for the four years following Tom's death, she had not even been exposed to other school children over that time, save for the cousins and old pals who swarmed to Fenwick each summer, and the occasional intrepid beau. Now she dreaded the kind of social pressure she had previously known at the Oxford School, "where there are always people who make you feel like an idiot." Whether out of inborn shyness or profound egomania, as her father believed, Kath knew she would never be "one of the girls."

Lugging her suitcase, Kath passed by the snarling stone lions standing guard at McBride Gateway on her way to Pembroke Hall. The medieval-looking, turreted dormitory was actually two buildings—"Pem West" and

"Pem East"—connected by an enclosed archway that housed the dining room. The massive wooden doors paneled with opaque leaded glass were flanked by huge wrought-iron lanterns. Crouching above the doorway, four stone friars stared down benevolently at all who entered.

Kath's ground-floor room at Pem West ["First door on the right—a single big room, very grand . . . everything to build up my confidence"] was all her own; it is doubtful she would have had it any other way.

She had not yet discovered slacks. Keeping in mind Dad's theory that anyone who owned more than two suits or two pair of shoes at any one time was a "fop," Kath kept her wardrobe simple: "I had a French blue skirt, with buttons down the front, and what was then called an Iceland-knit sweater. I wore it all the time. That's all I had." It was the outfit she wore when she made her first appearance at the Pem West dining room. After a slow, "agonizing" entrance, Hepburn later recalled, "I could hear the voice of one of the most sophisticated, marvelously sure-of-herself girls saying, 'Self-conscious beauty!' Well, I wasn't a beauty but I sure was self-conscious! I went in and sat down—and practically never went back." For the next seven months, either her friend Alice Palache Jones brought food up to her room or she dined alone in restaurants. "I spent all of my allowance," she says with a sigh, "eating out."

Kate describes her freshman year at Bryn Mawr as "agony." "It was agony for me even to go to the bathroom," says Hepburn, explaining why she would get up at 4 A.M. to shower alone. "I was petrified all the time, but I somehow didn't create that impression. I was a very good athlete, but I didn't dare try out for anything, so I just pretended I was awful."

In class, she *was* awful. Being "totally absent in the head in chemistry," Kathy finally came to the realization that a pre-med major was out of the question.

Her classmates may have shunned her initially (she did not help matters by repeatedly forgetting the names of the few friends she did make), but the faculty "was wonderful. The professors had an enormous effect on me. They were kind and they were interested in kids finding their way." For a while, she flirted with the idea of majoring in psychology. "There was a Professor Leuba who was head of the psychology department," she recalls, "and he suggested the courses for me to take." She finally settled on majoring in world history.

No longer obligated to become a doctor, Kath was free to fantasize about a career. "Know what I want to be when I get out of college?" she told one classmate she had started warming up to. "An actress." There was a pause as Kath's new friend looked her over, then burst out laughing. "You?" she roared. *"You?"*

From then on, Kath kept her dream to herself.

Even with the question of her major settled, Kathy's grades in her first two years at Bryn Mawr continued to slide—perhaps because she was expending so much energy on extracurricular activities of her own choosing. Since her classmates were intent on casting her in the role of campus oddball, she was more than willing to play the part. She swam nude in the fountain of the library Cloister ("It's true. Now I don't know why I did that. The truth is . . . I'd spend the night in the library, get exhausted, then dip into the Cloister pool in a mad effort to stay awake. It was an act of the greatest virtue . . .") She also stood naked on the roof during a blizzard, and had an attention-grabbing habit of bursting late into class, much to the consternation of her instructors. Throughout her sophomore year she wore a threadbare green overcoat held together with a safety pin, and appeared to have surpassed all previous antics by having herself photographed nude in her room at Pem East. When the local drugstore owner got a glimpse of the negatives, he was so shocked that he declined to print them. Kathy laughed in his face.

Kathy's experience as "a great second-story man" came in handy with her move from Pem West to a second-story tower room in Pem East—"the first door on the left as you leave the dining room." Immediately, Kathy began to circumvent the posted 11 P.M. curfew by returning after hours via the ivy-covered trellis outside her second-story dorm window. She was never caught. Instead, her downfall came when she was discovered in a stairwell, smoking a scented cigarette. "I never smoked because I was so healthy," she recalls. "But somebody had a pack of perfumed cigarettes, and they gave me one and I lit it and smoked it and was seen and suspended for a week."

Kathy survived her suspension for smoking, but late in the fall of 1926 she faced another crisis that threatened to cut short more than just her academic career. On a weekend visit home, she suddenly doubled over in pain

---

213

and was rushed to the hospital with a severe appendicitis attack. At the time Kathy, desperately unhappy over her "dismal" grades, thought "Thank God, I hope I'll die."

With his daughter being prepped for an emergency appendectomy, there was no question in Dr. Hepburn's mind who would be doing the surgery. "Dad operated on me," says Kate, "much to the horror of the medical profession. It wasn't against the law [to operate on a relative] but was against custom. He couldn't have cared less." When one physician warned Hep he could be kicked off the hospital staff if he dared pick up a scalpel to operate on a family member, he shot back "To hell with the rules. Nobody operates on my daughter but me. Besides, I'm the best damned surgeon this hospital has got!"

The operation was anything but routine. Kath's appendix was so badly inflamed it would surely have burst and possibly killed her had surgery been delayed even another thirty minutes. Still, says Kate, "Dad got me up the day I was operated on, and home after only four days." Dr. Hepburn's insistence on getting patients up and about a short time after surgery—standard medical practice by the 1980s—raised eyebrows in the 1920s. "They used to keep you in bed for ten days with appendicitis, no matter who you were," notes Kate. "Dad performed a lot of prostate surgery on old men, and he'd get them up the day it was done. The hospital authorities said, 'You know, if this patient dies, we're going to accuse you of murder.' Daddy said, 'That's okay.' He knew he was doing the right thing. He had the courage of his convictions."

Kath recovered fully, but by the end of her sophomore

year her grades had not. She flunked College Latin, and did only marginally better in most of her other courses. There seemed little hope of her ever catching up. Dean Manning wrote the Hepburns and, according to Kate, "suggested that maybe it would be a good idea if I didn't try to continue college. They said they didn't know what was wrong, but that college wasn't working out." Hep's reply: "If I had a patient who was very ill, I sure as hell wouldn't release him from the hospital." Miss Hepburn stayed.

No one could have been more grateful for the second chance. "I was really on the point of being thrown out," Kate says, "and I thought, 'Oh, God, I don't want to be thrown out.' " She had finally decided that, if she was ever going to stop being an "embarrassment" to her family, an entirely new strategy was in order: "Hard work, and lots of it. Before, I'd go sit next to my friend Palache [Alice Palache Jones] in the library and study, and I could hear her brains going around and I'd die of jealousy. So I dropped her and sat next to a real slow brain."

Kath attacked her studies so ferociously in her junior year that the campus physician told her on two occasions to slow down. She did not, and the results were startling. By the end of the first semester she had pulled her grades up to honors level. "I discovered that although I wasn't that brilliant, I could do it—if I worked. You can do anything, anything in the world if you try hard enough. You've just got to keep on struggling, because everybody gets discouraged, and almost everybody quits, and there are a few who don't—and then they go on and discover gold." Her interests, Kath discovered, were more literary than historical; in her junior year she switched majors one final time—from history to English.

Kath's academic comeback might never have happened had Bryn Mawr been coeducational. "It would have been impossibly distracting," she now says. "It's a very pleasant pastime—the pleasantest—but I don't understand the current coed system at all. It's a ridiculous time to throw boys and girls together and then expect them to study! I was a monk back then."

Kath continued to dream of a career on the stage, though now, since that humiliating incident back in her freshman year, she stayed mum. Her newly respectable grade-point average made Kath eligible for the College Varsity Dramatics group. She donned white pants, tie, and navy blue blazer for her first part—the lead role of Oliver in A. A. Milne's *The Truth About Blayds*. Some valuable coaching came from speech professor Samuel Arthur King. ("He was a hangover from the days of M. Carey Thomas, who cared desperately how people sounded. Most people make an unattractive noise when they open their mouths, and this is too bad. I learned then to speak with a certain amount of confidence.")

To add further authenticity to her portrayal of a male, she chopped off her long, straight red hair, parted it on the left, and plastered it down with brilliantine. "I thought," she says, "that I made a damned attractive young man."

The production ran two nights—April 8 and 9, 1927—and a week later the seven-woman cast traveled to Manhattan, where they gave a performance at the Colony Club to benefit the New York Alumnae Regional Scholarship Fund. Kath grew so fond of the charade that one night she boarded a train for New York and the Academy of Music wearing her male attire. Passengers did not quite know what to make of this androgynous creature. When she reached for change to pay the conductor, "I put my hand in my pants pocket and sat down and I couldn't get my hand back out!" She managed to pay her fare only after a struggle, leaving everyone no less confused.

24.

I was totally unaware that
we were the second-rate sex.

In her junior year, Kath was now a star athlete, both a trophy-winning golfer and a member of Bryn Mawr's 1927 championship swim team. But her reputation as the campus misanthrope was hard to shake, and her only close friends were four other misfits who, for reasons never entirely clear even to Kate, referred to their little cabal as "The Tenement." ("I felt safer with them. Safety in numbers.")

After her impressive junior-year comeback, Kath decided to reward herself with a trip to Europe. Alice Palache Jones went along. "I had accumulated some money, $500, by picking potato buds," Kath's friend recalled. For her part, Kathy said she'd hock her mother's furniture if she had to. Before his daughter could implement that scheme, Dr. Hepburn grudgingly anted up a matching $500. The girls paid $210 each for the roundtrip fare to Plymouth, where they rented bicycles. "But we hadn't figured on England being so hilly," said Palache, who split off from Kath for a couple of days to meet up with her again in Cambridge. Kath waited at the station for her friend, and Palache would remember her "running along the railway platform when she saw me on the train." In London, the two Americans were strolling down Great Portland Street when they came across "a very nice man called Mr. Seymour" who sold them a used Morris for a bargain price of 95 pounds—$475 according to exchange rates then. Their expenses—two shillings and sixpence per night, plus gas—came to a sobering $5 daily.

Kath and Palache scrimped on meals and for a time even considered sleeping in the park or in public buildings. "Damn this trip!" cursed a fed-up Hepburn.

Her friend was equally perturbed. "We are *not*," she chimed in, "going to stay in those musty old cathedrals."

Kath went back to the "very nice" Mr. Seymour and tearfully pleaded their case in what Alice Palache Jones would describe as an Academy Award-caliber performance. Mr. Seymour bought the Morris back for "practically no less" than what the Bryn Mawr girls had originally paid him for the car.

From there, Kath and Palache journeyed to France, where Hepburn's most vivid memory is of a young Englishman at a Left Bank café "waving his arms trying to get across what kind of chicken he thought he wanted." Kath's own fluency in the language improved, she says, due to the fact that "there was always a bottle of wine on the table. In England we'd been nonalcoholic, because of the expense."

Kath's senior year. The final stretch. She continued to apply herself and to spread her wings as an actress. Kath's second role before a paying audience was that of Theresa in Bryn Mawr's Christmas season production of G. Martinez Sierra's *The Cradle Song*. Although the *College News* spelled her first name "Katherine"—a mistake to be repeated hundreds if not thousands of times over the course of Hepburn's career—its review was memorable if only for the following two sentences:

> Katherine [sic] Hepburn, as Theresa, was so extraordinarily lovely to look at that it was difficult to form any judgment on her acting. Her voice had, perhaps, too much of the childish treble, but her little movements, her poses,

and the contrast of her gaiety with the re-
strained atmosphere of the convent, could not
have been improved.

The paper reserved its most lavish praise for a fresh-
man. "By far the best piece of acting," said the *College
News*, "was Margaret Barker's interpretation of Sister
Joanna of the Cross."

"We had some very good actors," Hepburn recollects.
"I was not, I think, one of them. Margaret Barker was
very good. She was absolutely fascinating. And Maggie
Hupfel [who had a small part in *The Cradle Song*] was
brilliant. She was tall, and this was before the onslaught
of the giant ladies; I was considered very tall in those
days and she was much taller than I was."

Two months later, Kath tagged along to a Yale party
with one of her Fenwick girlfriends and met a handsome
graduate art student named Bob McKnight. Dancing
away the evening, she felt unusually comfortable in
McKnight's arms.

"What are you going to be?" she asked.

"I'm going to be the greatest sculptor in the world,"
answered McKnight, a descendant of the illustrious
sculptor John Quincy Adams Ward and the noted genre
painter Edgar Melville Ward. "Now, what about you?"

"I am going to be," she replied without a moment's
hesitation and in dead earnest, "the greatest actress in
the world."

Kath half expected him to laugh, but he didn't. Smitten, he accepted her invitation to spend the Easter holidays with the Hepburns in Hartford.

Like many guests before him, McKnight found the

conversational free-for-all at the dinner table and the Hepburns' laissez-faire attitude toward him rather intimidating, and he did not leap headlong into the frank discussions about contraception and Communism. But the Hepburns doted on all artists, and the young sculptor was no exception. (Within a decade, Robert McKnight would be awarded the Prix de Rome for his sculpture. He later became director of the Memphis Academy of Arts.) Clearly they were fond of him, though Kath seemed to be keeping her distance. As he watched her dash back and forth from the kitchen, eating and talking and laughing with the others, he had no way of knowing what feelings, if any, she had for him.

McKnight bunked with Kath's two brothers that night. The next morning, he awakened to a torrid kiss from Kath, who fled almost before he knew what had happened. Catching his breath, McKnight turned to see Bob and Dick still tucked in their beds, fast asleep.

#

Dad thought acting was sort of a cheesy way to make a living.

Graduation was only six weeks away, and Kath was still just a face in the crowd. That changed with Bryn Mawr's quadrennial big May Day, an event M. Carey Thomas herself had initiated in 1900. This two-day-long Elizabethan extravaganza, featuring maypoles, masques, revels, and a half-dozen plays of the period, was originally conceived as an alternative to the boy-girl social dancing forbidden by the Quaker faith. Bryn Mawr students donned armor and chain mail as well as diaphanous gowns and lady-in-waiting attire. "It was enormous, beautiful," one alumna recalls of the festival. "Only thing wrong was that there weren't any real men!" Actually, young male faculty members, most of them single, did dress up in full Walter Raleigh regalia. They were referred to as "the Temptations."

May Day's *pièce de résistance* this year was to be a production of John Lyllie's three-act pastoral *The Woman in the Moone*. Kath's long red hair and flamboyant looks made her a natural for the lead part of the mercurial Pandora.

"The play had not been done since it was written in 1597," says Hepburn, and indeed, the program described *The Woman in the Moone* in the archaic style of its period, as

> a lively fantasie, shewing much learning, writ
> by the Euphuist John Lyllie, Maister of Artes,
> as it was presented before her Highnesse, im-
> printed at London for William Jones, and sold
> at the Signe of the Gun, neere Holburne Con-
> duict, 1597.

> If you would learn why the moone is ever in-
> constant and fickle this play will teach you; and
> you will see the woman who doth make it so.
> Pandora, as nature hath made her, is pleasing
> in every way, but the Planets each one give
> her his own humor for a time, so that she is
> sometime sullen, sometime vain, and some-
> time martial.
>
> It is for the first time played by these players
> and has not been shewn for manie a long
> yeare.

Kath had her own strong ideas about the role of Pandora; she insisted on playing her not as some wispy,
fragile creature but rip-roaring and barefoot, as the author originally intended. Her old psychology professor
Dr. Leuba allowed Kath to use his office as her dressing
room, and as the players assembled for the procession
that would lead along a graveled path beneath the arbor
to the Cloisters, a member of the faculty urged Kath to
put on sandals; once they had reached the lawn where
the play was to be performed, she could remove them.
But Kath was adamant. This was, after all, the same girl
who had run smack into an oak to show any doubters
just how tough she could be.

Kath drew on her mother's passion for this performance, playing Pandora as a firebrand and rebel and,
in the process, eclipsing her fellow actors. When it was
over, the audience of students, faculty, and parents
thundered their approval. "I was just thinking about

---

myself," Kate says, trying to recall her triumph. "I can't talk about it because I didn't see it, but I guess I was the brilliant feature."

One who did see it was a man named Jack Clark, who lived in a house adjacent to the campus and was watching from his back porch as Pandora made her entrance, her sleeveless white gown and firecracker-red mane blowing wild in the breeze. After the play, Clark rushed up to congratulate Kath. "He was a very handsome man," says Kate, "and he was quite interested in the theater." Pandora perked up considerably when Clark mentioned that he was a good friend of a young theatrical producer named Edwin H. Knopf, whose brother Alfred happened to be in the publishing business.

"Eddie Knopf had a stock company in Baltimore, where my Aunt Edith and the Hookers lived," Kate recalls, "so I planned to go down there with my letter of introduction and see if I could get a job."

Before that opportunity, however, Bob McKnight invited her to picnic outside the small Connecticut town where he had attended prep school. He had something he wanted to show her, something he shared with no one else: his secret rock overlooking a pristine pond. This was the spot where he sorted out his problems and pondered the future, and where he intended to ask Kath to marry him.

McKnight *intended* to ask. Instead, he sat in total silence while she carried on a nonstop monologue about how "thrilling" life was turning out to be, how endless the opportunities unfolding before her. Whether or not she was intentionally trying to head off a marriage proposal, that was the result. Her soliloquy ended abruptly at 6, at which time Kath kissed McKnight and announced that it was time to depart. (The encounter on McKnight's rock may, after all, have had some lasting effect on Hepburn. Kate once confided to me that she has her own "secret spot" in Central Park where she has studied for all her parts since the 1930s. The spot is near a rock, overlooking a small lake.)

Three weeks before graduation, Kath decided it was time to call on Eddie Knopf. Another member of the Tenement had, unbeknownst to her parents, secretly purchased a car six months earlier, and Kath had helped her keep it hidden. It would be available to her. Kath was not about to ask Dad for gas money, so she telephoned McKnight at Yale. His ten-dollar money order arrived at Bryn Mawr the next morning, and that afternoon Kath pushed her way past a secretary into Knopf's office at Baltimore's Auditorium Theater. She thrust Jack Clark's letter of introduction under Knopf's nose and waited for the producer-director to say something.

Knopf hardly knew what to make of this "awkward, green, freaky-looking girl" with orange-red hair pulled back into a "charwoman's bun" and a scrubbed-raw face glistening with sweat.

"He took one look at me," Kate recalls of the encounter, "and said, 'Well, you write me when you are through with college.' " She then asked if she could at least stick around and watch Knopf direct. Absolutely not.

When she finally agreed to leave, Knopf felt "only one reaction. I was glad to see the last of her."

Kathy had other plans. "Dad always said if you want to accomplish something, don't phone, don't write—go in person. They can throw a letter in the trash but they can't do that to you!"

Four days before graduation, Kathy returned to Baltimore and the Auditorium Theater, again unannounced. This time no one was in Knopf's office, so she went back outside into the street and reentered the theater through the front door. Rehearsals were in progress. Knopf was sitting in the orchestra, giving direction and taking notes. Kath slipped into a seat in the last row ("It was a huge theater") and watched. Over the next couple of hours, Kathy noticed actors disappearing into the wings. Around lunchtime, Knopf leapt onstage and seemed to vanish as well. Kath stayed put; she assumed that Knopf was working backstage with the cast and that in order to leave the theater they would all have to walk right by her. "I did not," she admits, "even know that there was such a thing as a stage door. Thought the actors had to walk out through the exit doors or the lobby like everybody else."

It was several hours before Knopf reappeared ("I waited and waited and waited and waited until I thought I was going to die if I didn't go to the bathroom"), and when he did Kath was ready to pounce. But before she could, "Eddie Knopf came back up the aisle and just walked by me and said 'Report for rehearsal next week.' And that was it." It would only be a non-speaking, walk-on role, but Kate describes that first professional job as "a wonderful part, a good little part, as one of six ladies-in-waiting in a comedy about Catherine that Great called *The Czarina.*"

Knopf (who would go to Hollywood later that year and would eventually write, direct, or produce twenty-eight films, including *The Santa Fe Trail* and *Lili*) had told the six girls to be there at 10:30 A.M. that first day to pick up their costumes. "So I thought, 'Hmm . . . 10:30. I better be there by 10:00 and get the best one. I got there at 10:00, all right—and all the costumes were taken. The others had all gotten there at 9:30." Then, "a miracle": One of the others walked up to Kate, the most beautiful court costume draped over her arm.

" 'Look,' she said, 'I got here first, but I'm going to be married soon, and I think you're going to have a great future, and we're the same size, so'—she held the costume out to me—'here, you take my dress.' "

Years later, Kate would recall this as "one example of why I love the human race. Now the horrible thing is, I just said, 'Thank you very much' and took it right from her. And that's how I got started."

Graduation Day, 1928, a Saturday in June. The Bryn Mawr gymnasium was packed literally to the rafters— half the guests were forced to look down on the proceedings from the overhead running track that encircled the gym. Dr. and Mrs. Hepburn, who had taken the train down from Connecticut, had no difficulty spotting their daughter: Kath's mannish stride was unmistakable as she made her way up to the stage to collect her diploma.

To Hep, Kath's graduation with honors constituted irrefutable proof that, with a sufficient degree of application, any goal was attainable. For Kit, still striking at fifty, the day brought back a flood of bittersweet memories—of her own parents, gone for so very long now, and of a deathbed promise kept. Nor could Tom have been far from his family's thoughts; before his life had been so brutally and senselessly cut short, it was his graduation from Yale that Hep and Kit had expected to attend first.

Kath had only one thing on her mind: how to break the news to Dad, who viewed actors with utter contempt, that in two days she was committed to start rehearsals for her first professional role. By the time she slid behind the wheel of her friend's car to drive her parents home to Hartford, she still had said nothing. It was not until she had driven for forty-five minutes along Route 202, as far as Doylestown, Pennsylvania, that she finally worked up the courage to blurt out the news.

"I've got a job, Dad. I'm an actress. Eddie Knopf has a wonderful stock company in Baltimore, and he's hired me to act in a play called *The Czarina* . . ."

Kath's father stared blankly at her. Surely she wasn't serious.

". . . and I start day after tomorrow, Monday."

Dr. Hepburn was furious. Kit sat silently in the back seat while her husband flew into the kind of black rage that had made him Nook Farm's legendary spanking dad. Acting was silly, pointless, egocentric. Besides, as Kate would admit, he "didn't think I had a prayer of making it as an actress."

White with rage, Dr. Hepburn demanded that Kath stop the car. "Let me out!" he shouted. "I'll take the train!"

Kath tried to calm him down by explaining that she had merely chosen to follow in Mother's footsteps. Hadn't Hep been willing to watch his wife "perform" on the socio-political stage for years, even encouraged her to stir thousands of people to action? Hadn't he approved when Tom, Kath, and the other kids joined Kit's supporting cast on picket lines and the lecture circuit?

That was all for the public good, he exploded. "This," he snarled, "is nothing but your vanity."

The argument raged for hours, until finally Dad reached into his wallet and grudgingly handed her fifty dollars—his bridge winnings, he took pains to point out—for the trip to Baltimore. It would, he expected, cover two weeks' living expenses—"enough to last until you recover from this madness."

The sun shone with particular brightness that Sunday morning in West Hartford. Kath lugged her battered suitcase out to the car, stuffed it in the trunk, and slammed the lid. The entire household stood on the porch to wave goodbye: Bob, Dick, Marion, and Peggy were there. So was Fanny Carrier, and Kit, of course. And Dad.

Kath turned to wave goodbye. From this moment on, she would hear the name Kathy less and less. Tomorrow her fellow players in Baltimore would start calling her Kate ("As in *The Taming of the Shrew?*" someone would jokingly ask).

"You'll be back," Dr. Hepburn called. "You just want to show off and get paid for it!"

Sixty years later, Kate Hepburn reflects on that moment. "Of course," she says, "he was right."

Epilogue

"You never really *know* anybody, do you? I never really knew Spencer, not really. I was very, very close to my Mom and Dad, but I'm not certain I knew them." As shockingly contradictory as this might sound—particularly in view of the depth of her relationships with Spencer Tracy and her own parents—I understood precisely what she meant as we talked in her New York townhouse in early 1988. Her commitment to these three individuals was total, and yet doubts remain, questions are left unanswered—questions that never will, never can be answered. "We all say, 'I'm going to put this piece of me in a little box and I'll never let anyone see it—not anyone.' "

It took years for Dr. Hepburn to arrive at the conclusion that, just maybe, his daughter had chosen the right profession. "He thought acting was kind of a cheesy way to make a living," she said, "and he thought I wouldn't last. The first salary I got from movies—I threw it all in a bureau drawer and then spent it. He had to pay my taxes! After that, he just put me on this allowance. And I've been on an allowance ever since."

Once her father had grudgingly accepted his daughter's chosen vocation, however, Kate never doubted his intense interest in her work. One of her first roles on stage was the lead in *Death Takes a Holiday*. She was fired after just a few performances. "I got absolute opposite reviews from different papers," she remembered. "One critic said that I was this adorable, Maude Adams-type creature. The other called me a 'skeleton with a rasping voice.' So I was either one or the other. Terrible."

It was at such times that Kate could turn to Dad for an honest (sometimes brutally so) appraisal. "After I was

233

fired, my father came backstage and told me I gave 'a splendid performance of a neurotic jackass.'"

"I said, 'What do you mean, Daddy?'

" 'An eighteen-year-old girl dumb enough to go off with Death is certainly a neurotic jackass. That's the way you played it.'

"And I said, 'Well, now I know why I was fired.' "

Kate counted on her father's candor and took it as a sign of his pride in the quality of her work. Kit, of course, was supportive from the start, and once the children were all grown and her placard-waving days by and large behind her, she became increasingly involved in Kate's career, accompanying her daughter on tour and on rare occasions even discussing some of Kate's movie projects with members of the press. Whenever a houseguest might summon the courage to point out that Kate had starred in a turkey or two, Kit could be counted on to haul out her scrapbook full of glowing reviews and prove the naysayer wrong.

Yet more and more, Kate was nagged by the feeling that perhaps her mother did not entirely approve of the direction her movie-star daughter's career had taken; the Hepburn films that delighted the moviegoing public may have seemed to Kit a little too frivolous, too lacking in social relevance. Kit's own tastes ran to the classics and to the avant-garde.

As a result, Kate wonders occasionally whether she may not have missed a higher calling. "Sometimes I think I'm wasting my time in the movies," she told me, "and should be out trying to do something to get us back on the right track." In other words, she wonders if perhaps she shouldn't have followed in her activist mother's footsteps. (Hepburn's own top social priority is education. "The really big problem is the decline of the system, with people who can barely read getting into college.")

Losing her mother in 1951 came as a shock to Kate, not just because it was so unexpected, but because, like Tom's death, it changed the dynamics of the family that had always been her refuge. A few months after Kit's fatal heart attack, Dr. Hepburn married Madelaine Santa Croce, his longtime nurse and a family favorite for years. Far from being resentful that her father had remarried so soon after Kit's death, Kate was grateful. "Well, when you've had a wife for forty-five years, I suppose it's pretty hard to get along without one," she confided to a friend at the time. "I like Santa—she'll be fine for Dad. We all should be damned grateful to her—she's taking on quite a handful." Kate has only fond words for Santa, who remains very much alive. "So you still technically have a stepmother?" I asked. "Oh, yes," Kate replied, as if it were the most natural thing in the world.

Dr. Hepburn died at his home ten years after Kit, on November 20, 1961, with Kate and the rest of the family at his bedside. "Dad died when he was eighty-two. He would have lived longer," she told me, "but he didn't like medical doctors, he just liked surgeons, so he diagnosed himself. He thought he was having a heart attack, but it turned out what he really had was a gall bladder that burst. And that really downed him." Ultimately, he succumbed to lobar pneumonia. Hep was buried alongside Kit and their son Tom in the Hepburn family plot at Hartford's Cedar Hill Cemetery.

Upon the death of both her parents, "Aunt Kath," as

she is known to a battalion of nieces and nephews and grandnieces and grandnephews, assumed the mantle of leadership in the family. While these Hepburn offspring have fanned out across the continent, little seems to have changed in the lives of Thomas and Kit Hepburn's children. Dick, the nonconformist experimental playwright whom Garson Kanin recalled as wearing bright red pajamas to the theater, lives year-round at the house in Fenwick and plays host to Kate during summers and weekends. Harvard-educated Robert is the only Hepburn to fulfill his father's dream, having served as director of the urology department at Hartford Hospital until he retired to his West Hartford home in 1973.

While Bob followed in the late Dr. Hepburn's professional footsteps, it was Marion who came closest to emulating their mother. Marion attended then-progressive Bennington College in the 1930s, and at seventeen spent the summer between her freshman and sophomore years working for pioneer social worker Jane Addams at Hull House in Chicago. The next summer, Marion took a job in the Washington office of John L. Lewis, the legendary head of the United Mine Workers union. After marrying Hartford's Ellsworth Grant, Marion concentrated on writing books about Connecticut history. The Grants' daughter pursued an acting career of her own under the name of Katharine Houghton. She is best known for her role as the daughter of the characters played by Katharine Hepburn and Spencer Tracy in their last film together, *Guess Who's Coming to Dinner*.

With Marion's passing in 1986, the eldest Hepburn remains close to the youngest, her startling lookalike,

Peggy. "Noel Coward took one look at her," Kate recalled of an evening a half-century before, "and said, 'Now that's what Kate *should* have looked like!' " Peggy is a librarian at the Canton Public Library in Collinsville, Connecticut, a ten-minute drive from West Hartford.

Katharine Hepburn's body of work, stretching over six decades and encompassing the worlds of theater, film, and television, is without equal. A truly great talent may be born or perhaps simply emerge as the product of a unique environment. Either way, Kate Hepburn, the American original, knows what she owes to her parents. "What those two people did for me," she said, "*is* me. I could never repay them."

Acknowledgments and Sources

This biography is in itself a tribute to its subject and to her marvelous and unique family. If that is not sufficiently obvious, then I must state my thanks to Katharine Hepburn for her wisdom, her example, her bountiful memory, and, most of all, her friendship. I am also immensely grateful to my editor, Donald Hutter, for his skill, vision, and support, and to another friend—Ellen Levine, who happens to be a marvelous agent as well.

While Kate and a number of her contemporaries I spoke to were the most reliable eyewitnesses to many of the events described in this book, there was still plenty of digging to be done. For their help in this enterprise, I am indebted to (in no particular order):

Homer Dickens; Ben Carbonetto; the Bettman Archives; the late Marion Hepburn Grant; the *Hartford Courant* and the *New York Times*; Rob Kyff of the Kingswood-Oxford School; Caroline Rittenhouse and the staff of the Bryn Mawr University Archives; Corning Corporate Archives Director Stuart K. Sammis; Gerard J. Shorb and the staff of the Alan Mason Chesney Medical Archives at Johns Hopkins University School of Medicine; Nancy B. Newins and the staff of the Randolph-Macon College Archives; Laura Vassell and the staff of the Stowe-Day Foundation; Gus Johnson; the Connecticut Historical Society; the staffs of the Hartford and West Hartford public libraries; the Buffalo and Erie County Library; the Corning Public Library; the Woodbury, Connecticut Public Library; Hartford Hospital; St. Paul's Parish of Hanover County, Virginia; the Silas Bronson Library; the Connecticut State Library Archives; Radcliffe College; Smith College; Yale University; the University of Hartford; Harvard University; and the Lincoln Center Library for the Performing Arts.

As she has been for more than sixteen years, my wife Valerie was a wellspring of faith, humor, and encouragement—qualities she has passed along to our daughter, another young Kate.

The following publications also provided background material for the book:

Bacall, Lauren. *By Myself*. New York: Alfred A. Knopf, 1979.

Bryan III, J. and Lupton A. Wilkinson. "The Hepburn Story." *The Saturday Evening Post*, Nov. 29, 1941.

Collier, Christopher, with Bonnie B. Collier. *The Connecticut Scholar: The Literature of Connecticut History*. Middletown, Conn.: Connecticut Humanities Council, 1983.

Crofut, Florence S. M. *Guide to the History and Historic Sites of Connecticut*. Vol. II. New Haven: Yale University Press, 1937.

Dickens, Homer. *The Films of Katharine Hepburn*. Secaucus, N.J.: Citadel Press, 1971.

Dreiser, Theodore. *A Gallery of Women*. New York: Horace Liveright, 1929.

Falk, Candace. *Love, Anarchy, and Emma Goldman*. New York: Holt, Rinehart and Winston, 1984.

Gilliatt, Penelope. "Miss Hepburn," *Vogue*. November, 1981.

Gilman, Charlotte Perkins. *The Living of Charlotte Perkins Gilman*. New York, 1935.

Goldman, Emma. *Living My Life*. New York: Alfred A. Knopf, 1931.

Grant, Marion Hepburn. *The Fenwick Story*. Hartford: Connecticut Historical Society, 1974.

————. *In and About Hartford: Tours and Tales*. Hartford: Connecticut Historical Society, 1978.

Gray, Madeline. *Margaret Sanger: A Biography of the Champion of Birth Control*. New York: Richard Marek Publisher, 1979.

Horowitz, Helen. *Alma Mater*. New York: Knopf, 1984.

Jensen, Oliver O. "The Hepburns." *Life* Magazine. Time Incorporated, 1940.

Kanin, Garson. *Tracy and Hepburn*. New York: Viking Press, 1971.

Kaplan, Justin. *Mr. Clemens and Mark Twain*. New York: Simon and Schuster, 1966.

Kingswood Oxford Today, Commemorative Issue 1909–1984. West Hartford, Conn.: Kingswood-Oxford School, 1984.

Mackenzie, Midge. *Shoulder to Shoulder.* New York: Alfred A. Knopf, 1975.

Merrill, Arch. *Southern Tier.* Interlaken, NY: Empire State Books, 1986.

Schorer, Mark. *Sinclair Lewis: An American Life.* New York: McGraw-Hill, 1961.

Warner, Charles Dudley. *My Summer in a Garden.* Boston: Houghton Mifflin, 1871.

A Hepburn Family Chronology

1852   Amory Houghton, Sr. (Kate's maternal great-grand-father) establishes the Union Glass Company in Somerville, Massachusetts.

1864   Amory Sr. sells the Union Glass Company and moves to Brooklyn, New York. There he establishes the Brooklyn Flint Glass Company with himself and eldest son Amory Jr. (Kate's great-uncle) as principal owners.

1867   Fire sweeps through Brooklyn Flint Glass.

1868   Amory Houghton, Sr. and sons Amory Jr., Charles, and 17-year-old Alfred Houghton (Kate's grandfather) move to Corning and establish Corning Glass.

   The Reverend Sewell Hepburn (Kate's paternal grandfather) moves from Missouri to Hanover County, Virginia to become rector of St. Paul's Episcopal Church. He marries Selina Lloyd Powell of Richmond.

1874   Alfred Houghton leaves Corning and the family glass industry to start his own firm, the Buffalo Scale Company, in Buffalo, New York.

1878   On February 2, Alfred Houghton and Caroline Garlinghouse Houghton become the parents of Katharine Houghton (Kate's mother). From infancy, she is known as Kit. (Kit's two sisters soon follow—Edith in 1879, Marion in 1884).

1879   Thomas Edison approaches the Houghtons of Corning to design a bulb for the first electric light. Corning will be the leading manufacturer of light bulbs for the next century.

1892   Kit loses both parents. Alfred Houghton shoots himself at age 42 over business losses and his wife's cancer. Caroline succumbs to her illness days later. She is 33.

Kit, now 14 years old, leaves Buffalo with her sisters to live with their uncle Amory Houghton at his mansion in Corning.

1895   Over Uncle Amory's initial opposition, Kit makes good her deathbed promise to her mother and enters Bryn Mawr College (to be followed by Edith and Marion).

1896   The Reverend Sewell Hepburn's son Norval Thomas Hepburn (Kate's father) enrolls in Randolph-Macon College in Ashland, Virginia.

1899   Kit graduates from Bryn Mawr and enters Radcliffe.

1900   Tom Hepburn graduates from Randolph-Macon and enters Johns Hopkins School of Medicine.

Kit earns a master's degree in art from Radcliffe.

1901   Kit moves to Baltimore, where Edith is a student at Johns Hopkins, and takes a job tutoring. She meets Tom Hepburn at a fencing match.

1904   Tom graduates from Johns Hopkins and in November marries Kit Houghton. They move to Hartford, Connecticut, where he joins the staff of Hartford Hospital as an intern.

1905   On November 8, Kit gives birth to their first child, Tom. As will be the case with all their children, he is given the middle name of Houghton.

Dr. Hepburn sets up his own pioneering practice—urological surgery as a medical specialty.

1907   On November 8, exactly two years to the day after the birth of Tom, Kit gives birth to a daughter. They name her after her mother: *Katharine Houghton Hepburn.*

1909 Kit Hepburn attends speech by militant British suffragist Emmeline Pankhurst. Dr. Hepburn urges his wife to join the movement. Kit forms the Equal Franchise League, precursor of the League of Women Voters.

   The Hepburns move into Hartford's Nook Farm district, home to such literary lights as Harriet Beecher Stowe and Mark Twain.

1910 Dr. Hepburn enlists the support of George Bernard Shaw in publishing and distributing Eugène Brieux's controversial play about venereal disease, *Damaged Goods*, and convinces noted American educator Charles Eliot to join in establishing the American Social Hygiene Association.

   Kit becomes close friends with Pankhurst, and as one of the country's leading crusaders for women's rights comes in contact with social reformer Charlotte Perkins Gilman, anarchist Emma Goldman, and other radical figures of the day.

   Kit, Kate, and her brother Tom encounter President Woodrow Wilson while picketing the White House.

1911 Kate's younger brother Dick is born, followed by Bob (in 1913), Marion (in 1916), and Peggy (in 1918).

1912 The Hepburns buy a rambling seaside "cottage" in Fenwick, Connecticut.

   Kate joins her brother Tom at Hartford's West Middle School.

   Kit attacks Hartford's booming white-slave trade.

1916 Nine-year-old Kate stars in a backyard performance of *Beauty and the Beast*.

1917 Kit resigns as head of the Equal Franchise League, which she founded, throwing her weight instead behind the more militant Women's Party of Alice Paul.

1918   Kate is enrolled at the private Oxford School in West Hartford.

1921   On the morning of April 3, while visiting a family friend in New York, 15-year-old Tom hangs himself. Kate, 13, discovers the body.

Unable to cope with school following her brother's death, Kate from now on will be taught at home by a series of private tutors.

The Hepburns move to a mansion on Bloomfield Avenue in West Hartford; Kate and her parents are befriended by new arrival Sinclair Lewis. Dr. Hepburn provides Lewis with much of his background material for *Arrowsmith*.

1922   Kit finds another cause. Teaming with birth-control advocate Margaret Sanger, she becomes a founder of Planned Parenthood.

1923   Kate wins her first state junior golf championship.

Kate begins her "career as a second-story woman," breaking into vacant homes in Hartford and Fenwick.

1924   Kate enrolls at Bryn Mawr.

1927   Kate acts in her first college production, A. A. Milne's *The Truth About Blayds*.

1928   In a senior May Day production of *The Woman in the Moone*, Kate stars in the role of Pandora.

Kate graduates from Bryn Mawr with honors.

Over her father's objections, Kate lands her first professional acting job as one of six ladies-in-waiting in a Baltimore stock production of *The Czarina*.

1928   On December 12, Kate marries Ludlow Ogden ("Luddy") Smith. They separate after a few weeks, remain good friends.

1941   Kate begins her 26-year personal and professional partnership with Spencer Tracy.

1951   Kit Hepburn dies of a heart attack at 73.

1961   Dr. Hepburn dies of pneumonia. He is 82.

1967   Tracy and Hepburn make their last film together *Guess Who's Coming to Dinner*. Two weeks after completion, on June 10, Tracy dies of a heart seizure.

1981   Carrying on her mother's fight for birth control, Kate lends her personal prestige to Planned Parenthood.

1986   Marion Hepburn Grant, Kate's younger sister, dies.

1988   On March 14, Kate attends a gala at New York's Waldorf Astoria launching Planned Parenthood's Katharine Houghton Hepburn Fund, so named in honor of both mother and daughter.

Index